The
Empress
Has No
Clothes

The Empress Has No Clothes

Conquering
Self-Doubt
to Embrace
Success

BK

Berrett–Koehler Publishers, Inc.
San Francisco
a BK Business book

Berrett-Koehler Publishers, Inc.
235 Montgomery Street, Suite 650
San Francisco, CA 94104-2916
Tel: (415) 288-0260 Fax: (415) 362-2512 www.bkconnection.com

Ordering Information

Quantity sales. Special discounts are available on quantity purchases by corporations, associations, and others. For details, contact the "Special Sales Department" at the Berrett-Koehler address above.

Individual sales. Berrett-Koehler publications are available through most bookstores. They can also be ordered directly from Berrett-Koehler: Tel: (800) 929-2929; Fax: (802) 864-7626; www.bkconnection.com

Orders for college textbook/course adoption use. Please contact Berrett-Koehler: Tel: (800) 929-2929; Fax: (802) 864-7626.

Orders by U.S. trade bookstores and wholesalers. Please contact Ingram Publisher Services, Tel: (800) 509-4887; Fax: (800) 838-1149; E-mail: customer.service@ingrampublisherservices.com; or visit www.ingrampublisherservices.com/Ordering for details about electronic ordering.

Berrett-Koehler and the BK logo are registered trademarks of Berrett-Koehler Publishers, Inc.

Printed in the United States of America

Berrett-Koehler books are printed on long-lasting acid-free paper. When it is available, we choose paper that has been manufactured by environmentally responsible processes. These may include using trees grown in sustainable forests, incorporating recycled paper, minimizing chlorine in bleaching, or recycling the energy produced at the paper mill.

Library of Congress Cataloging-in-Publication Data
Roché, Joyce M.
 The empress has no clothes : conquering self-doubt to embrace success / Joyce M. Roché ; with Alexander Kopelman. -- First Edition.
   pages cm
 Includes index.
 ISBN 978-1-60994-636-4 (pbk.)
 1. Self-doubt. 2. Self-evaluation. 3. Success. I. Title.
 BF697.5.S428R63 2013
 650.1--dc23
                          2013005552

First Edition
18 17 16 15 14 13   10 9 8 7 6 5 4 3 2 1

Cover design: Irene Morris
Cover art credits: Desk and office © Dimitry Kutlayev/123RF;
  Woman behind desk © Eric O'Connell/Photolibrary/Getty Images
Book producer and designer: Detta Penna
Copyeditor: Kirsten Kite
Proofreader: Katherine Lee

I dedicate this book to the incredible women who are
or have been a part of my life, beginning with
my mother and my Aunt Rose
and including
my biological sisters
and the dear friends who are as close as sisters.

You have given me the strength to go beyond
what was expected, supported me in whatever path
I have taken, laughed and cried with me,
and have always been my biggest cheerleaders.
I am what I am today because of you.

Contents

Foreword

I wasn't surprised when I heard that Joyce was writing a book with the idea of helping younger people deal with this thing called the impostor syndrome. I've known Joyce for many years and have always admired her for her compassion, courage, and generosity. I have also been personally inspired by her life's story, so I was touched and honored when she asked me to write the foreword to this book.

I've had a pretty successful life and career by most measures, but there is still many a day when I get out of bed in the morning and feel like I am just not sure I am up to the task. There's this nagging doubt in the back of your mind that says, "Maybe I don't know this as well as somebody else. Maybe I'm just a fake."

I think that most people feel this way at one time or another. It's just that nobody talks about it. That's why I was so pleased when Joyce first started speaking publicly about these feelings she's had, and why I think this book is so important. In my time as CEO of a couple of large corporations, what I've become absolutely convinced of is that every business is a people business. And no business can really flourish if your people aren't comfortable in their own skins.

You are not going to know everything as well as the next person. And in any new job, you're probably going to feel like you are drinking from a fire hose for a while. But if you relate to people, if you help create an environment where they are important and accountable, they are going to give you all of the education you need and odds of success increase greatly.

When I look at my life, I know that was what allowed me to do the things I've done. And if I can do it, anybody can do it. I grew up in Ennis, Texas, a town of five thousand at the time, south of Dallas. My dad was a blue-collar union guy. He drove the trains for Southern Pacific railroad. My mom was a housewife. Dad didn't finish high school and Mom dropped out of college after one semester. I was a pretty average student and had no idea what I wanted to do, but Mom made sure I stayed in school and went to college.

I went off to Texas Tech, which was a state school, for the best of reasons: I had two or three friends who went there and tuition was seventy-five bucks. I got an engineering degree because I had heard most of my life that engineers get good jobs and I was pretty good in math.

From college, I went right to Southwestern Bell Telephone Company as an outside plant manager. Talk about feeling like an impostor. I was all of twenty-two years old and had this crew of veterans working for me, about eight or ten of them. That was when I learned the most important lesson of my career. Not only did I think I didn't know anything, but I was shy to boot. All I wanted to do was to hide out in my office and try to bone up on the things I didn't understand.

Well, the guy who was the manager for my department (he was my boss's boss) must have noticed. He came down one day and said, "C'mon, I want to look in on your crew." We drove out to where they were working. We got out of the car and were just starting to look around. I got to talking with the men, turned around, and my boss was gone. The message was pretty clear, but the next day he made sure I got it. "You have to be out with your people," he told me, "instead of sitting in the office." I never forgot that lesson and have throughout my career made it my highest priority to get to know the people I work with.

And what I discovered was that it helped me deal with my own self-doubts, especially as I advanced and eventually became a CEO; I wanted a company that was sort of a family. It was just my personality, but it also worked okay for me from a business perspective. At AT&T, it helped me build a company, and at General Motors, it helped me rebuild one.

When I went over to GM, on day one I went down to the company cafeteria, sat at a table right in the middle, and ate lunch. For two or three days, I ate alone in this place with maybe a thousand or two thousand people around me. They just didn't know what to make of my being there. By the fourth day that changed and I started to get what I needed to know to get the work done. We'd have lunch and I'd say to people, "How are things going? Tell me about what you are doing." You learn a whole lot more that way than looking at a bunch of slides and numbers all day. And then people start to believe they are a vital part of the business—and they are.

You know, I am an engineer, so over the years as I dealt with challenges, I often would write down my good points and my bad points on a sheet of paper. The bad points far exceeded the good ones for a long time. But no matter what, I always had confidence in my ability to get along with other people. And I guess after a time, I learned to get along with myself as well. It's not that I didn't feel uncertain of myself or even like an impostor in new situations; it just took less time to find my balance and to give myself credit.

I never had one great mentor, but I learned from different

mentors and emulating people I admired. Eventually, you take all of that, put it in a washing machine, and you come out. You become your own personality.

Learning how to get along with yourself and others to accomplish the objective, I think, is what success is really all about. And it is something you can learn how to do. This great book is going to help a whole lot of people learn to feel successful.

Edward E. Whitacre, Jr.
Former Chairman & CEO, General Motors Co.
and retired Chairman & CEO, AT&T, Inc.
April, 2013

Preface

Right around the time I first began thinking about writing this book, I heard Cory Booker, the dynamic young mayor of Newark, New Jersey, speak about his vision of what young people need to succeed. I found the speech moving, especially when in summing up, Mayor Booker said: "You've got to learn to metabolize your blessings." It seemed as if he was at once describing my own journey to embracing success and pointing the way for all of us who have faced the kind of self-doubt that has made us feel like impostors.

The inability to recognize and celebrate our own strengths and accomplishments is at the very heart of what is known as the impostor syndrome—that feeling of being a fraud and not deserving of our success. We look at the objective evidence of our success, and all we can see is a false facade that will inevitably come crashing down, unless we work tirelessly to maintain it.

"There were times I remember," says Dr. Ella Edmondson Bell, Associate Professor of Business Administration at the Tuck School of Business at Dartmouth, "I felt like I was a con artist. I felt I was being something I'm not."

Too many of us fritter away too much time, talent, and emotional energy on hiding who we really are because we are afraid we will not be accepted or acceptable. One of the most devastating aspects of the impostor syndrome is that by its very nature it isolates us from other people and forces us to keep our innermost feelings secret.

I lived with the secret feeling of not fitting in and the fear of being discovered as not being up to the task for much of my professional life. I know full well how heavy a burden that secret is, and I know what a wonderful relief it is to open up and to begin to question the voice that keeps repeating "you are not good enough" and "you don't belong here."

This book is an invitation to everyone who suffers from impostor feelings to realize that you are not alone and to begin working toward embracing your success. The purpose is not necessarily to answer the question of why you feel this way but to focus on the fact that you do not need to allow the feelings to define your life. As I learned through my own journey, the essential work of managing and ultimately conquering the impostor syndrome lies in learning how to metabolize external validation to turn it into the core strength of internal validation.

The root causes of the impostor syndrome are complex and manifold. And so are the situations that trigger them. (Your answers to the questions about impostor feelings at the beginning of the book may give you a glimpse of your own experience.) In the coming chapters, I will share stories of key milestones in my life when the fears of being discovered as a fake were particularly strong. Each chapter will focus on specific panic points, the times when my heart started to race and I was gripped with fear. Situations that I know will speak to some of your own experiences.

In each chapter, you will also hear the voices and stories of a group of some of the most amazing and successful people I know (both men and women), all of whom have dealt with the impostor syndrome, even though you never would have known it as an observer.

Throughout the book, I suggest strategies from my own experiences and those of others that you can use to begin to wrestle with your own sense of being an impostor. You cannot silence panic; you can only calm it. The best way to do that is to open up, at least to yourself, and to take an honest assessment of how you got to the place where you are and ask yourself whether you deserve to be there—in other words, to exercise the muscles of internal validation. The more you learn how to own your success, the more you will thrive on it.

If there is nothing else you take away from the book, I want you to know that comfort does come with time. My wish for you is that this book will help you achieve it quickly.

Do You Feel Like an Impostor?

If you are like most people, this might be the first time you are hearing the term *impostor syndrome*. We all feel uncertain of ourselves to some degree or another at times. The impostor syndrome, however, is a much more complex phenomenon than simple insecurity. The sample test (excerpted from the comprehensive test developed by Dr. Pauline R. Clance, the psychologist who has pioneered research and treatment of the impostor syndrome) will help you glimpse the feelings triggered by the impostor syndrome and see whether you have experienced them. Please keep in mind that this is not in any way a diagnostic test. The full test is available on Dr. Clance's web site paulineroseclance.com.

Sample Impostor Phenomenon (IP) Test

There are individuals who consistently demonstrate a high level of success, but who fail to incorporate their competency into their identity. In spite of very real achievements, these persons experience an inordinate fear of failure.

For each question, please circle the number that best indicates how true the statement is of you. It is best to give the first response that enters your mind rather than dwelling on each statement and thinking about it over and over.

From *The Impostor Phenomenon: When Success Makes You Feel Like A Fake* (pp. 20–22), by P. R. Clance, 1985, Toronto: Bantam Books. Copyright 1985 by Pauline Rose Clance. Reprinted by permission. Do not reproduce without permission from Pauline Rose Clance, drpaulinerose@comcast.net.

1. When people praise me for something I've accomplished, I'm afraid I won't be able to live up to their expectations of me in the future.

1	2	3	4	5
(not at all true)	(rarely)	(sometimes)	(often)	(very true)

2. At times, I feel my success has been due to some kind of luck.

1	2	3	4	5
(not at all true)	(rarely)	(sometimes)	(often)	(very true)

3. Sometimes I'm afraid others will discover how much knowledge or ability I really lack.

1	2	3	4	5
(not at all true)	(rarely)	(sometimes)	(often)	(very true)

4. When I've succeeded at something and received recognition for my accomplishments, I have doubts that I can keep repeating that success.

1	2	3	4	5
(not at all true)	(rarely)	(sometimes)	(often)	(very true)

5. I often compare my ability to those around me and think they may be more intelligent than I am.

1	2	3	4	5
(not at all true)	(rarely)	(sometimes)	(often)	(very true)

6. If I am going to receive a promotion or recognition of some kind, I hesitate to inform others until it is an accomplished fact.

1	2	3	4	5
(not at all true)	(rarely)	(sometimes)	(often)	(very true)

Scoring the Impostor Phenomenon Test

The Impostor Phenomenon Test was developed by Dr. Pauline Rose Clance to help individuals determine whether or not they have IP characteristics and, if so, to what extent they are suffering.

After taking the Impostor Phenomenon Test, add together the numbers of the responses to the six statements. If the total score is 12 or less, the respondent has few Impostor characteristics; if the score is between 13 and 18, the respondent has moderate IP experiences; a score between 19 and 24 means the respondent frequently has impostor feelings; and a score higher than 24 means the respondent often has intense IP experiences. The higher the score, the more frequently and seriously the impostor phenomenon interferes in a person's life.

Chapter 1

Breaking the Silence

The impostor syndrome, at its core, is a distortion in the way we see ourselves. The trouble is that we believe the warped image to be reality—the "truth" we've somehow managed to hide from the rest of the world. We are petrified that we will be discovered and spend nearly all our energy guarding against that possibility.

One of the most difficult aspects of the impostor syndrome is the fact that it demands that we keep our feelings a secret. Don't stay silent. Find a way to speak about your fears. Whether you do it with a trusted friend, a coach, a mentor, your partner, a therapist, or in a journal, give voice to all the feelings churning inside. (Writing to yourself can be one of the most effective methods to face the impostor syndrome. It was for me and many others.)

I looked out the wall of windows of my corner office at the masts of the tall ships tied up at South Street Seaport and at the span of the Brooklyn Bridge just beyond. Cool, wintry early-morning sunshine filled the large room. The city was waking up but still quiet. And I had the entire office and the next hour and a half to myself.

"I have the best job in the world," I said out loud, filled

with the contented knowledge of being in just the right place at the right time. I had been President and CEO of Girls Inc., the nonprofit organization dedicated to inspiring all girls to be strong, smart, and bold, for just over five years and was more excited than ever to get up every morning and go to work. Helping hundreds of thousands of girls shape their futures went way beyond job satisfaction, it fed my soul. At long last, I felt like a real success.

It had not always been so. In over twenty-five years of singular achievements in corporate America, I had risen to unprecedented heights for an African American woman, becoming the first to be named an officer of Avon Products, a Fortune 500 company. Just about every new accomplishment, however, came with the stultifying doubt that I did not deserve the success and that sooner or later I would be discovered as an impostor.

I glanced at the book galleys on my desk. The journalist and author Ellyn Spragins had asked me to contribute to her book *What I Know Now: Letters to My Younger Self* and had just sent me the proofs as the book neared the final stages of production. I picked up the galleys and reread the letter addressed to Joyce at thirty-three.

Dear Joyce,

You may not have set out to be a pioneer, but here you are, out front, one of the few African American women working up the corporate ladder. You achieve more every year, but each leap exerts more pressure. Who would have thought success could feel so much like a burden?

Yes, you thrive on it. You love marketing, and the more you

work, the more you're consumed and fascinated by it. Here at Revlon, you're setting a personal record, working morning till night—and both days on weekends. Exercise? Forget about it. You can't even plan a lunch, because chances are a meeting will be called at noon.

You're not complaining, because, strangely, there's a giddiness in such hard work. You risked a lot every time you seized an opportunity that presented itself. Laboring ever more intensely shows you're worthy of the chances you've been given. It also props open the door for every African American woman who might be coming behind you.

This is what you tell yourself—and it's all true. But it only goes so far. The way you drink up that steady stream of praise and recognition is a tip-off. You did a good job. You belong here. We want to make you an officer of the company.

Ever wonder why the glow wears off so soon? Because somewhere, deep inside, you don't believe what they say. You think it's a matter of time before you stumble, and "they" discover the truth. You're not supposed to be here. We knew you couldn't do it. We should have never taken a chance on you.

The threat of failure scares you into these long hours. Yet success only intensifies the fear of discovery.

Stop. It. Now. You're not an impostor. You're the genuine article. You have the brainpower. You have the ability. You don't have to work so hard and worry so much. You're going to do just fine. You deserve a place at the table.

And at the end of it all, people will remember you not for hours you worked but for the difference you made in the world.

Love,

Joyce

That letter was a turning point for me. As I had thought about it, an odd phrase kept popping up in my mind: "The Empress has no clothes. The Empress has no clothes." It was so strange and seemingly out of context. But it was insistent enough that I thought I had better pay attention to whatever its message might be. The only thing I could think of was to go back and reread Hans Christian Andersen's *The Emperor's New Clothes*, in which the Emperor really has no clothes.

What I—as most of us, I think—remember about the famous fable was that the vain Emperor goes parading through his realm naked because neither he nor any of his people want to admit that they cannot see the new "suit" the grifters posing as weavers had "made" for him. What struck me now, however, was the clothes' purported magical quality: "[The weavers] proclaimed that they knew how to weave cloth of the most beautiful colors and patterns, the clothes manufactured from which should have the wonderful property of remaining invisible to everyone who was unfit for the office he held, or who was extraordinarily stupid."

In the story, it is the fear of being seen as unfit for one's office or as being stupid that keeps everyone, except an innocent child, silent. I recognized that fear immediately as the one I had encountered so frequently throughout my life—the terror of being unmasked as an impostor "unfit" for my post. I thought about all the times that fear had kept me from speaking out, had insisted that I work twenty-hour days, had whispered in my ear that I did not deserve the promotions and recognition. "They'll find you out," it kept saying. The letter for Ellyn's book came straight from all those memories and a newfound confidence to confront my fear of being an impostor.

That quiet morning in my office, as I took in the words, I felt a new sense of pride. I had not only succeeded in spite of all these fears, I had learned how to quiet them enough to enjoy my success.

I leaned back in my chair and looked at a brightly colored tugboat guiding a barge downriver. In a wink, I was transported back home to New Orleans, a young girl watching barges carefully threading their way along the Industrial Canal. I could almost smell the diesel of the tugs mixing with the heavy scent of Mississippi river mud as I crossed the bridge that divided the Ninth Ward from the rest of the city.

I was just a year old, the youngest of nine children, when my mother moved the family from our hometown of Iberville, Louisiana, to New Orleans after my father was killed in a hit-and-run accident. She had two older sisters in the city, neither of whom had children of their own, and figured that raising us kids would be a whole lot easier in a place where she could get steady work and help looking after us. By the time I was old enough to remember, our household spanned between Mama's house and Aunt Rose's house a few blocks away.

Neither Mama nor Aunt Rose had gone beyond the eighth grade in school because they had had to go to work. However, they reminded us every day that education was our ticket to doing more in life, to getting beyond the limitations other people would try to put on us. This was the South in the 1950s, mind you, so, as young African Americans, there were lots of limitations we had to face.

"Joyce Marie," I heard Aunt Rose's familiar voice in my mind, "if you work hard and study, there is nothing in this world that can stop you. Get an education, and you can make something of yourself."

As I surveyed my life on that bright New York morning in 2005, I knew that Aunt Rose and Mama would have been proud—much more so of the person I had become than just of the things I had accomplished. And I wondered why it had taken me so long to become proud of me and to trust that I was worthy of success.

I flashed on the exact moment I became aware of the change, when I felt more confident and comfortable with my success. After nearly two decades at the company, I had risen to the post of Vice President of Global Marketing at Avon. And I was doing a great job, leading the establishment of the company's first global marketing organization and creating strategies that generated close to a billion and a half dollars in worldwide sales. In spite of that, when a position with even more responsibility became available, I was passed up for the promotion. Needless to say, I was not happy. I had encountered the proverbial glass ceiling on several occasions before, but this time, rather than doubting myself, I decided to embrace my success and to step out and believe in my abilities. I knew I deserved that position. Somehow, without even realizing it, I had internalized my success as something I had earned. It was as if a spell had been broken.

I had traveled so far in my thoughts, I was a little startled when I heard Yolanda, my executive assistant, say, "Good morning, Joyce."

The workday had begun, and I would have to return to exploring thoughts about the meaning and the price of success at another time.

I had occasion to revisit this theme in just a few short months, when my letter, along with two others, was excerpted from Ellyn's book in advance of publication in *O* Magazine, in early 2006. The calls, e-mail messages, and letters started coming in immediately. Their volume only increased when the book came out in April. Everyone, it seemed, from young women just entering college to male CEOs of blue-chip companies, wanted to talk about their own fears of being unmasked as impostors.

My very personal reflections had struck a raw nerve for thousands of people. By their very nature, impostor feelings tend to keep people silent. They are secret fears that we are lacking in some way. Who wants to admit to not being worthy of their post, right? But they are also a terrible burden to carry around by yourself. So when they read my letter, people wanted to talk, to share, to get the weight off their chests.

One of the most surprising conversations I had at that time was with Ed Whitacre, former chair and CEO of AT&T, on whose board I served. Ed was as buttoned-up as they come, and was someone whom I felt could not possibly have any self-doubt. So I was more than a little taken aback when he came up to me after a meeting and said, "Great letter, Joyce. And a brave thing to do. But you know, that feeling you describe, it doesn't affect just women and minorities. I've had my share of moments when I felt people would find out I didn't make the grade." I could see in his eyes that he had shared something with me he had not told very many others and nodded my acknowledgement. With that, he moved off to shake hands around the board table.

Through all the conversations I have had, I kept thinking what a shame it was that many smart, talented, accomplished people were so tortured by doubt they could not enjoy the success they worked so very hard to achieve. I knew firsthand how awful it was never to feel quite sure enough of yourself to relax, and I wondered what caused so many of us to feel such anxiety.

I heard the term impostor syndrome for the first time during a panel discussion in which I participated with two other women whose letters appeared in Ellyn's book, Eileen Fisher, the clothing designer, and Shannon Miller, the Olympic gymnast. During the question-and-answer session, a young woman directed a question to me: "Joyce, you spoke of the encouragement and support you got from your family. How do you reconcile that with the impostor syndrome you describe in your letter?"

"Well, it helped that I didn't know I had a syndrome," I joked. "Seriously, though, that's a great question. The support and encouragement gave me the strength to take the risks I took in the first place. Without them I would have just done what was expected. But that's the conundrum of this whole thing. I was the one taking the risks, and yet I felt as if I was only getting anywhere because somebody else was giving me a chance. And I had to work harder and harder to be deserving of those chances."

That evening, when I got home, I went online immediately and started searching for information. Now that I knew it had a name, I wanted to know what exactly the impostor syndrome was and what caused it.

I did find some references but very few, and all almost exclusively concerned with academia. The one I found the most fascinating was what I later learned was the seminal article on the subject published in the fall of 1978, in the journal *Psychotherapy Theory, Research and Practice,* by two psychotherapists, Pauline Rose Clance, Ph.D and Suzanne Imes, Ph.D, "The Impostor Phenomenon in High Achieving Women: Dynamics and Therapeutic Intervention."

The article, based on the doctors' work with "over 150 highly successful women," defined, for the first time, the impostor phenomenon:

> Despite outstanding academic and professional accomplishments, women who experience the impostor phenomenon persist in believing that they are really not bright and have fooled anyone who thinks otherwise. Numerous achievements, which one might expect to provide ample object [sic] evidence of superior intellectual functioning, do not appear to affect the impostor belief.

The authors went on to describe the experiences of these women, suggest possible root causes of the phenomenon, and propose ways to treat it. Although I identified with many of the feelings the women described, frankly, I found some just too extreme to be believable, like the insistence of a woman with "two master's degrees, a Ph.D, and numerous publications to her credit" that she was "unqualified to teach remedial college classes in her field." I had to remind myself to remain kind, calling to mind the kinds of mental gymnastics I had resorted to over the years to keep believing my success was a fluke.

And then I got to the last sentence, which described what happens when a person lets go of her impostor feelings: "She begins to be free of the burden of believing she is a phony and can more fully participate in the joy, zest, and power of her accomplishments." Wow, I thought, that is how we all ought to live, with joy, zest, and power. I just kept repeating those three words: Joy, zest, and power. Joy, zest, and power. And every time I said them, I felt like doing a little dance.

But it was another line from the article that really lodged itself in my soul: "If one woman is willing to share her secret, others are able to share theirs." I had seen just how eager people were to unburden themselves, and I began to hear a call. People started suggesting to me that I write a book based on my own experience with the impostor syndrome and that of the people who had responded to me. What appealed most to me about this idea was the prospect of helping thousands and thousands of people break the silence that makes the impostor syndrome such an isolating and heavy burden. I knew firsthand how liberating it was to let go of the secret and to speak of the fear out loud, and I wanted to pave the way for others to shake off their stultifying secret so they could start enjoying their success earlier in life than I had.

Eileen Fisher, founder of the iconic clothing company, Eileen Fisher Inc., found that comfort as she developed effective strategies for quieting the voices that say, "You are not good enough. You don't belong here." Eileen launched her business in 1984, with $350 in savings and a desire to create simple clothes that make the woman important, that let her relax into herself. She is now the chief creative officer of the $300 million employee-owned company.

In our conversation, Eileen spoke very movingly about her own path of overcoming the feeling of being an impostor and her wish for her own children and all young people to learn how to be comfortable with who they are as human beings.

Eileen Fisher: *Relaxing Into Ourselves*

I grew up in the Midwest, in a suburb of Chicago called Des Plaines, the home of McDonald's. I am from a family of six girls and one boy. My dad used to say jokingly that children should be seen and not heard, and that was pretty much the idea. My parents weren't stern or anything. It was just that our opinions didn't matter, and we weren't drawn out. We were part of a bundle of kids.

My mother was overwhelmed by the kids, the house. Our general idea was to hide from her, stay out of the kitchen, stay out of her way, just be invisible and avoid what we used to call "ranting and raving."

We were a Catholic family, so I went to Catholic school for twelve years. There, if you stepped out of line a little bit, you got yelled at. And so you just always kept yourself small, tried not to be seen.

So none of us kids ever stood out or gave our opinion. We had this desperate need to fit in. I spent my life as a girl trying to make myself small—not seen and not heard.

At the same time, I must have had some need to break away, because I wanted to go to college. That was kind of a shock to my father. He said, "I'm glad, but we don't have the money to send six girls to college. I'm saving the only money we have for your brother."

I put myself through college at the University of Illinois and ended up with a degree in home economics. After that, I moved around a bit. There weren't very many jobs in the seventies.

I finally came to New York, with my Midwestern portfolio and my home economics degree, trying to be an interior designer. It was a hard, hard road. I worked in interior design and graphic design, but

I didn't feel like I was a real designer. I sort of felt like an impostor. I struggled getting clients and getting jobs and projects. I don't think I would have been able to get a job as a clothing designer. I had to start my own company to believe in myself.

The amazing thing is that even as I became successful, I kept getting this message from people around me that I was the last person they expected to do well. What kept me going was the sense of rightness I felt once I started the clothing business. It wasn't just about business, it was about making something that made women feel good, about clothes that created confidence. I felt I had found my spot, and that gave me validation.

I began to develop confidence in myself as a designer, to believe that I understood something meaningful and that I had a talent. But I didn't have confidence in me. I wasn't at all sure I was OK.

I found communicating with people especially hard and began to realize I was not going to succeed if I had to explain my designs all the time and negotiate about why this one was better than that one. Even today, I am still terrified of standing in front of groups and speaking. I guess it throws me back to my childhood, when I was not supposed to be heard, when it was important to be invisible because someone might not like you.

As I've gotten older, though, I don't feel like I have to know everything or be everything. But I did spend many years in therapy—along with journaling, yoga and meditation—to get here. And I keep up my meditation practice, and I find that it really helps me stay centered on a daily basis.

I think a lot of us build our careers believing that titles or money will help us get respect. And they do, to some extent. But professional success can leave that hole there right in the center of who you are, that missing sense of I'm just OK.

The message I want to give people—what I would have wished for myself—is that the most important thing you can do is work on your core personal confidence as a human being.

If people understand and are comfortable with their essence, they are able to do many more wonderful things. I feel like I'm just coming into my sense of myself and realizing that I'm more than a clothing designer, that I can have a joyful life, that I can contribute to the world in lots of different ways—supporting leadership in women and girls is just one of them. I'm getting to that place of really feeling comfortable and confident about who I am. It's just taken so long. I feel like I went the roundabout way. And I would like it to be different for my son and my daughter and young people everywhere. I want them to work on who they are as human beings rather than what they do.

I invite you to entertain, for a moment, the possibility that the way the rest of the world sees you—as competent, knowledgeable, accomplished, and successful—is actually more accurate than the way you see yourself. It is difficult, I know. But if you can tolerate the discomfort, you will probably glimpse the kind of joyful life Eileen describes. After many, many years of struggling with the anxiety of feeling like an impostor, I assure you that such a life is well worth the effort required to gain a more balanced view of yourself.

Chapter 2

It's Not What You Wear

Those of us who experience the impostor syndrome tend to evaluate ourselves against a very narrow range of criteria that have more to do with our sense of how we do or do not fit in. Become familiar with your impostor. Think about the situations that trigger your impostor fears. In what ways do you feel different from the people you compare yourself to and how do you go about trying to fit in?

Ask yourself: "What am I trying to prove? To whom? And why?"

One of the most vivid memories I have from my early childhood is of playing in the backyard of my Aunt Rhodie's house. As I mentioned earlier, after my dad died Mama moved to New Orleans to be near her sisters, Rose and Rhodie. We all lived a few blocks from each other in the Carrollton section of New Orleans, not too far from Xavier University. The flat we lived in was small. With seven of us—Mama and six kids who still lived at home—it always felt crowded. Aunt Rhodie's backyard had room to breathe, and it had a couple of trees to play under. To me, it was an oasis, and I would spend hours there.

My brothers had fixed up a makeshift swing on a tree from a length of rope and a tire. Mama thought it was way too dangerous for anyone under ten, and I was strictly admonished to stay off it. Of course, you can't keep a kid off a swing. The adults were out working during the day, and my older siblings, while trying to be conscientious about keeping an eye on the younger kids, couldn't stand guard over me at all times. So I got a fair amount of swinging in on the sly.

My secret came out in very dramatic fashion. One day—I must have been in first or second grade—I came home after school and headed straight for the swing. It was a hot day and the idea of the wind carrying some of the stickiness away from me as I swung sounded really good. As I started pumping my legs, I paid no mind to the jagged remnants of a low limb that had snapped off in the last big storm. I was so carried away by that wonderful sensation of flight you get as you gather momentum on a swing, that it took me a couple of seconds to register the sharp pain in my leg. I looked down in a daze at the big hole the broken branch had punched in my leg. And then I started bawling—as much out of pain and fear as out of anticipation of the hell I expected to catch for disobeying.

Mama was so relieved that I wasn't hurt even worse, that she went fairly easy on me. My siblings, though, got much stricter marching orders to keep me in line. For a while, it felt as if I did have my very own bodyguard.

I am not sure I knew it at the time, but I was incredibly fortunate to have sisters and brothers who took such good care of me. Lillian, the oldest, who is seventeen years my senior and was already married and out of the house, regularly came over on weekends and took me downtown, to stroll on Canal Street, shop at Krauss, or get a soda at Woolworth's. Those trips were much more than just much-needed outings; they were an education on how to make my way in a racially segregated world. Back in our neighborhood, everyone was Black. We had our own stores and our own schools. Our teachers were Black, our doctor was Black, and our postman was Black. We didn't see white people much, and we didn't have to keep out of their way.

All that changed, though, the moment you got on the streetcar to go downtown. To this day, if you get on the St. Charles line—the oldest in New Orleans—you can see the slots in the tops of the seats that were used for the wooden screens that separated the whites from the Blacks. We could move the dividers to within two rows of where any white passengers sat, but we had to sit behind the screen. And once we got downtown, there were separate eating counters, and if you wanted to buy clothes, you were not allowed to try them on before you paid for them.

Our families and our community handled the prejudice and injustice as African Americans had always done, with an unswerving determination to protect us kids physically and emotionally and to instill in us the belief that we could aspire to happy, productive lives. The message we got from all the adults in our lives—parents, teachers, community elders—was, "Work hard, respect yourself, aim as high as you can."

As I entered elementary school, the civil rights movement was still in its early days. I was in first grade when the Supreme Court unanimously voted for school desegregation in *Brown v.*

Board of Education. Emmett Till was murdered in Mississippi the August I was getting ready to start third grade; and Rosa Parks sparked the Montgomery bus boycott that December.

I don't remember having been aware of any of these events, but the adults around me certainly were. They knew that my generation would have unprecedented opportunities, and they worked even harder to help us prepare to make the most of these opportunities. The message drilled into me at home and at school was that education was the way to rise above our circumstances and to succeed. I took that message to heart and worked really hard to do well in school.

Ours was a big, fluid family. The house on Short Street where Aunt Rose and Uncle Charles lived was just a block or two away from Mama's house, and Aunt Rhodie and Uncle Joe lived around the corner. I started going back and forth between the three households when I was six. My older sister Doris had at some point started living full-time with Aunt Rose and Uncle Charles. I would spend many afternoons at their house and sleep over every so often. It was nice and quiet and a whole lot less crowded than Mama's flat.

I gravitated to the quiet and the extra attention. By the time my youngest sister, Sandra, was born the fall I entered third grade, I spent more and more time at the house on Short Street. And then one day, totally unawares, I simply didn't go home. It wasn't a big deal. There was no family meeting. I just now lived with Aunt Rose and Uncle Charles.

Uncle Charles worked as a mechanic at the Singer Sewing Machine factory; Aunt Rose worked as a domestic, like Mama. There wasn't a whole lot to spare, but they took me in as one of their own.

Aunt Rose and Uncle Charles expected us to work hard and behave. They set high standards for us, because they knew the obstacles we faced and the discipline it would require to get past them.

The Lower Ninth

When I was in fifth grade, Aunt Rose and Uncle Charles decided that it was time they owned a house. There were cheap lots available in the Lower Ninth Ward, and they went ahead and bought one. I'll never forget going down there to visit the place. Although the lot was right across from the new Joseph A. Hardin Elementary School, it looked like a swamp, with standing water covering much of the ground. Uncle Charles must have seen the look on my face and reassured me that the lot would be filled in and that indeed a house was going to be built on it.

Over the next year, we'd go down regularly to marvel at the wooden frame that was slowly going up and at the grass that was beginning to grow all around. It was really exciting to watch our new home take shape.

The house was finished, and we moved in the summer before I started sixth grade. It wasn't easy switching schools at eleven, but Hardin was a good place, and I adjusted. Unfortunately, it only went up to sixth grade, and the following year I went off to McCarthy School for two years of junior high. So I had to leave my brand new school to attend one that looked like it had been built in the last century, as it probably had. But it helped tremendously that right at the start of the year I met Barbara Ricard; we quickly became friends and have remained very close to this day.

The Ninth Ward was a much larger and more diverse area than Carrollton. It was still segregated, but Blacks and whites seemed to live much closer together. You'd have several square blocks that were white and then several square blocks that were Black. That also meant that school segregation was much more of an issue. McCarthy went up to eighth grade and, in those days, high school started in the tenth grade. In our area, there were no Black junior high schools, and, of course, we were not allowed in the white school that was nearby. For the next year, therefore, Barbara and I spent an hour each day on the school bus, riding all the way back to Carrollton to attend ninth grade at a Black school.

I was a pretty good student, and my academic ambition and hard work did pay off. I applied to and was accepted at McDonogh 35, the oldest Black high school in New Orleans. Established in 1917, the school had a well-deserved reputation for excellence. It was non-districted—any African American student from across New Orleans could apply—and quite small, with only about one hundred and twenty-five in my graduating class. Therefore, the application process was very competitive, and I was overjoyed to have been accepted.

Barbara had also gotten into McDonogh 35, and we spent the summer getting ready for the exciting social life of high school. She and I had learned to sew in home economics class and had a lot of fun competing over whose seams were straighter. (She usually won.) We'd spend hours poring over Simplicity patterns and then choosing fabrics. Since Uncle Charles worked for Singer, we had a good sewing machine at home, and Barbara and I made dresses and skirts. I even attempted slacks. By the end of that summer, we were ready.

The "35" admissions process was the first merit-based academic competition I had ever entered. It was exhilarating—and pretty intimidating—to think that I would be going to high school with some of the brightest kids from the whole city. This was a huge step toward my goal of pursuing a college degree at Dillard University.

In our family, Dillard was the epitome of "making it." Throughout my school years, a photograph of Aunt Rose and Uncle Charles on the Dillard campus had the place of pride at our house. Although they hadn't had the opportunity to complete high school, it was clear in the picture just how proud they were to be on the grounds of this institution of higher learning. For them, it was an expression of the aspirations they had for us kids.

I had the added motivation of having seen Doris go through her entire four years at Dillard and graduate with a degree in education. Visiting the campus with her gave me a sense of what college could be like, and I was determined to work harder than ever to make sure I would get there.

The End of Childhood

Everything changed just as I started tenth grade. Uncle Charles suffered a massive stroke and was in the hospital, paralyzed on the left side. For days and weeks, Aunt Rose and I spent hours at his bedside, helping him slowly fight back to regain some movement and control over his body. (Doris by now had married my brother-in-law Al, who was in the Army, and they were stationed in Virginia. So it was just Aunt Rose and me, with occasional help from the rest of the family.) We were told that Uncle Charles was lucky to be alive and that he would remain an invalid for the rest of his life.

When we finally brought Uncle Charles home, he needed constant care. Aunt Rose had to stop working to look after him, and we went from a two-income household of very modest means to one where three people had to get by on disability and public assistance. I knew that it was now up to me not only to take care of myself but also to contribute to the family in whatever ways I could. "Aunt Rose and Uncle Charles have done for you," I said to myself, "now it's your turn to help them." In my mind, even though I was only a teenager, it was time for Joyce Marie to become an adult.

In addition to taking on much more of the housework, I started working on weekends to bring in a little money. On Saturdays, we had another family member look after Uncle Charles, and Aunt Rose and I went out to do domestic work. I remember in particular this one woman for whom we cleaned. She was a writer for a magazine and always dressed in the most elegant clothes. And there we were in our work aprons. It was hard not to feel a little self-conscious.

I wasn't ashamed of working or of coming from a family that didn't have a lot, but I knew I was different. At McDonogh 35, the students came from families that represented the whole complex social order of the Black community in New Orleans. There were low-income kids like me. There were kids like Barbara from comfortable working-class families. And there were many from solidly middle-class and upper-middle-class families, whose mothers and fathers were the teachers and doctors we saw as role models of African American success. What set me apart from all of my peers, though, at least in my own mind, was that I had to be responsible for myself. After Uncle Charles's stroke, I couldn't burden the family with my needs, nor could I count on them to provide me with the support they had given me until then.

I began to feel anxious about my ability to make my way in the world and to succeed. Would I really be able to compete with all these smart kids whose families had so many more resources than mine did, whose parents could help with homework and hire tutors if they had trouble with a particular subject? If I managed to keep my grades up and get into college, how would I pay for it? Would I be able to continue my education and work at the same time? These were the questions that increasingly occupied my mind.

The weight of these adult concerns stamped me as different, and I went to great lengths to disguise that fact. I didn't want my friends and schoolmates to know that I was not like them. I wanted to be accepted as one of the crowd, to fit in, and pretended to be as carefree as my classmates. I kept up with cheerleading and participated in the school's social life. But I did all of these things with an underlying seriousness, with a special purpose and determination. I did them all wearing a mask. I kept my life of work and responsibility a secret so that I could appear to fit in.

Now when I sewed with Barbara, I still had fun, but in the back of my mind I also knew I was doing it out of necessity. When I made plans with friends, I also had to consider whether I would need to work that weekend. One incident has remained with me as an especially painful memory. *The Sound of Music* came out in late March of 1965 and became an instant sensation. My entire class was going to see it at a movie theater on Canal Street on a Saturday afternoon. Rather than admit that I couldn't go because I had to work, I insisted that I didn't want to see the picture. Of course, I was dying to see it, and the lie felt hollow and transparent.

The Seeds of Unease

As I have reflected on my experience with the impostor syndrome, I have come to believe that the days in high school, when I felt I had to hide my reality in order to fit in, laid the foundation for the fear of being discovered that haunted me for so much of my life. The disunion between the inside and the outside quickly became a burden in itself—a constant demand for vigilance to make sure that nobody would see that I was wearing a mask.

That felt like a really important realization. My impostor fears were as much about being discovered pretending to be someone as they were about failing at a particular task. In essence, what I had been afraid of for so long was that I would fail to maintain a convincing facade.

To understand this better, I asked Dr. Pauline Clance, the pioneer in impostor syndrome research, what she considers to be the difference between impostor feelings and insecurity. She explained that the impostor syndrome is much more complex and that through her clinical experience she has seen that people who suffer from the impostor syndrome tend to be very successful, whereas people with high insecurity tend to be less accomplished. One way to interpret this is that although impostor feelings certainly include questions about one's ability to compete, they are also about social standing and fitting in, while insecurity is primarily about one's abilities.

Paradoxically, the search for validation and acceptance drives people who experience impostor feelings to take on ever-greater challenges, to always reach for the next level, which then triggers the concerns about their ability to measure up. It's as if once we get on that treadmill, we find it very difficult to stop.

My good friend Janice Warne offers some really profound insights into the way in which anxiety about fitting in can trigger a lifelong battle with the impostor syndrome. I first met Janice when I joined Girls Inc. as president and CEO in 2000. At the time, Janice was managing director, fixed income at Salomon Smith Barney and a very dedicated and involved board member of Girls Inc. We hit it off right away and worked very closely together over the years, particularly after Janice became the chair of the board.

"Joyce, I think you and I were separated at birth," she often jokes. And while our backgrounds are as different in some ways as you can imagine, our experiences bear remarkable similarities.

Janice Warne: *The Luxury to Just Be Me*

I grew up in Westchester, a middle-class suburb of Los Angeles. I was raised quite conservatively in a Mormon household. My father was not a Mormon, but my mother was devout, so, in spite of my father's disapproval, my two older sisters and I were raised in the Mormon Church.

I went to public schools. The education wasn't rigorous, but it was fine, and I always got really good grades. My junior high and high school were very diverse, and I liked that.

Our house was not a happy place. My father was a very distant person, and he was pretty miserly. I honestly don't know how much money he did or didn't have, but I always felt like we weren't as well off as everyone else, that money was always an issue.

When my father left around the time I was a junior in high school, we really had money trouble. In the 1970s, alimony settlements weren't anything to speak of. Mom had about five thousand dollars in the bank and the house, and that was about it. So I didn't have any resources to fall back on.

At about the same time, I really started to question Mormonism, and particularly the way I felt it discouraged women from pursuing their dreams. I felt pressured to go to Brigham Young University to study, but the real purpose was to find a husband and start a family. Watching how my father left us with nothing, I knew I wanted to be self-sufficient. And I really thought I could achieve something—what, I didn't know. But I wanted to set my sights higher than just having college be a way station on the path to marriage.

My options for college, though, were limited to schools within California, thanks to a generous state scholarship. I applied to a couple of the University of California campuses, the University of Southern California, and Stanford, and Stanford gave me the most scholarship money. Even back then, they had need-blind admissions, so I was accepted based on my qualifications, not on whether or not I could pay.

Stanford was a wonderful, beautiful environment. But I really had a hard time in my freshman year and, frankly, probably through most of the years there. I didn't have that fun, freewheeling experience that my classmates had. Probably the biggest issue was that I was always really aware of the great economic divide. My freshman-dorm roommate had her own nice car and went away for weekends. Another person down the hall lived on Park Avenue. Most were well-traveled, and many had gone to private schools. And I, on the other hand, every quarter had to cobble together scholarships and work to stay in college. So I gravitated to a couple of African American guys at the dorm. I fit in better with them, because our economic realities were more similar.

The sense of not fitting in spilled over into the academic sphere and affected my self-confidence. Even though I did great in high school, I was really intimidated throughout college, because in a place like Stanford there are so many people who are incredibly brilliant. On top of that, I was working all the time, so I didn't have as much time to study, which just reinforced my worries about being able to make it.

The pressure took its toll. I kept thinking, "Are you good enough to compete? You are kind of always aiming at the top, and is that realistic? Is this self-deception?" I finished with a BS in earth sciences and completed an honors program in humanities. So, in spite of my difficulties, I did well at Stanford.

After college, I got a job with the City of Santa Monica, working with the redevelopment agency. The city was working on a bond issue with the investment banking firm of Blyth, Eastman, Dillon, and they called to ask me to interview for an associate position in the municipal healthcare group. I got the job and moved to San Francisco.

I did really well at Blyth and worked there for six years. In fact, I really flourished, loved the work, and was promoted to vice president. Although my colleagues thought I was crazy, I still felt like I needed a stamp of approval and thought I should get an MBA, just to have that on my resume. I applied to business school at Harvard and Stanford, got accepted to both, and ended up going back to Stanford.

I felt that now that I had done OK in the little pond of San Francisco, what I really wanted was to go into investment banking on Wall Street. I don't know why I thought I needed an MBA to do that or why it was important to me to set yet another difficult goal. Why move to New York? Why pick the highest bar? It seems that throughout my career I ended up doing that which exacerbated all the worries about my ability to fit in.

I signed on with Salomon Brothers out of business school and joined the financial institutions group, which had a reputation as one of the more difficult ones, both in terms of the work and the intensity of the people. And within the department, I joined the securitization effort, which was even more intense and round-the-clock. It was also highly quantitative, and although I know instinctively that I am good with math, there was no training in the analytics the group used. So when it came to the numbers, I worried I didn't know everything I was supposed to know. I just assumed that everybody expected me to know more than I knew, even though we had quantitative people supporting the work.

And although I went on to have a very successful career, being a great product specialist and managing very successful groups within my department, it seems there was always some aspect or area of the work that I felt like I ought to have known but didn't. And so I was never really able to rid myself of the doubts: Am I prepared for this? Am I ready? Am I able to do this? Yet I kept going into the tougher and tougher areas, and I have often wondered why I did that.

I think there was always this pull to prove myself. If I didn't do the hardest thing, I felt like I was copping out. But even as I succeeded, there was no respite. No matter how well I did, I think I went into the office every day feeling like I had to prove myself all over again.

All told, I was with the bank for twenty-one years before taking early retirement. There were aspects of the work that I loved, things I knew I excelled at, and many great colleagues. I also did very well and was one of a few senior women within my division. However, in my mind, I had to keep proving myself, and the only way to do that was in the toughest city, at the toughest firm, in the most difficult department, on the toughest product. That's a lot of pressure to put on yourself day in and day out. And now, I am not entirely sure to whom I was trying to prove myself or for what.

I do know that there has not been one day when I have missed being back at my old job. I can choose to work on projects or for causes I am passionate about, and I don't feel that I have to prove myself to anybody. It's wonderful to have finally let go of all that pressure I put on myself and to use that energy in a positive way. And I can just be me.

To quiet that voice of self-doubt you have to learn to accept yourself. That's much easier said than done, I know. But it can be done. Start by looking at your strengths and challenges as a whole person. What are the special skills you have? What are the qualities about you that attract others to you? What makes you the person you are?

Chapter 3

What If You Have No Silver Spoon?

One of the paradoxes of the impostor syndrome is that the people who suffer from it tend to be ambitious and accomplished. We are driven to succeed, and yet when we achieve the success we are seeking, we inevitably find ourselves out of our element, which results in new fears of being discovered.

Know your fear. Success puts us in unfamiliar situations, and it is natural to feel anxious. To feel that you do not deserve to be where you are, however, is quite different. Learn to distinguish between the stress of moving up into new levels of responsibility and influence and the conditioned response of impostor fears.

The civil rights movement was rapidly gaining momentum during my time in high school. In 1962, James Meredith enrolled in Ole Miss, causing widespread riots and leading President Kennedy to send five thousand Federal troops to Mississippi. As I started my junior year in 1963, Dr. King spoke of his dream for our nation to a crowd of more than two hundred thousand gathered in front of the Lincoln Memorial.

Our elders recognized that real change was on its way. And they encouraged us even more insistently to prepare, by excelling in school and going to college, to make the most of the opportunities that might be opening up for us. At the same time, the violent opposition to the civil rights movement was a constant reminder of just how enormous the obstacles we faced really were. I can still see the stunned faces of my classmates and teachers as we learned that President Kennedy had been shot. Although we didn't know what had really happened, in our hearts each of us sensed that the killing had something to do with us—with the profound and very fragile changes that were happening in our lives.

That November was a turning point for me. I was midway through my junior year and was now thinking about the future even more seriously. With the general sense of anxiety in the country and the financial pressures at home, it seemed to me that I had one shot to get things right. I needed to choose a path that would give me the best chance to succeed. I was good at math and got lots of encouragement from my math teacher, so I decided that I would study to become one myself. For a Black girl from a family of modest means, at that time in New Orleans, that was an ambitious goal, but an attainable one.

I also felt that I had to get realistic about what college I could attend. Dillard was my dream, but with Uncle Charles incapacitated and Aunt Rose taking care of him full time, the family simply didn't have the money to pay the tuition at a private school. I figured I could earn enough to pay my way at a state college and set my sights on Southern University at New Orleans. Barbara was planning to go there as well, and the prospect of being on campus together softened the disappointment of having to give up my dream.

Even though I was now working toward applying to a school with less demanding admissions criteria than those of Dillard, throughout the rest of junior year and all through senior year, I did not feel like I could ease up. Barbara still reminds me about what a serious student I was. And I was serious, because I couldn't afford to slip up. I felt that I had no safety net—no one to fall back on if I failed. I had to make good grades, to earn enough money to save for college, and to keep up the appearance of being a regular high school kid.

Senior year, I applied and was accepted to Southern and set about my preparations. Jobs were not easy to come by; as an African American woman you couldn't even work as a salesperson in a department store. So I did what I could, mostly domestic work on weekends and during vacations. The summer after we graduated, I tried my hand at telemarketing for a magazine, but I was terrible at it and only lasted a few weeks. But even with the occasional setback, I managed to save up the few hundred dollars I needed for tuition and books, for my first semester of college. By late August, I was ready and excited to start.

On August 29, we heard that tropical storm Betsy had become a hurricane and had passed Puerto Rico. Now in New Orleans, we were so used to storms, nobody paid them too much attention. For us kids, some of the big ones were sort of like snow days up north, we'd miss a day or two of school, but that was about it. So for the next week and a half, we went about our business, expecting that if it did come near New Orleans, Betsy would cause some minor inconvenience and move on.

We did put up some extra food and water on September 9, when the weather bureau in Baton Rouge warned that the storm was almost certain to hit the city. The wind and rain did get pretty intense by that evening, but even then we didn't think there was any real danger. I think I was already all tucked in bed when I heard knocking on the front door. It was one of our neighbor's adult sons. He was standing in about a foot and a half of water, and I could tell that it was rising pretty fast. The levees had been breached, he explained, and then said that he and his brother would help us get Uncle Charles across the street to take shelter at the school.

The school was already crowded, and more people were arriving all the time. It was only a one-story building, but there was a storage room on a second level. That's where we all huddled. But after a while, there simply wasn't enough space. At that point, several men used whatever tools were at hand to break through the roof, and those of us who could, climbed out and spent the night up there.

As morning broke, we began to get a glimpse of the extent of the destruction that had visited the Lower Ninth Ward. The lake had literally spilled into our neighborhood, and the school seemed to be floating, along with most of our houses, in deep water. Overturned boats, fallen trees, and utility poles drifted by. Overhead, helicopters circled slowly. Stunned, tired people raised their hands in greeting as they made their way past us in heavily laden boats.

Eventually, a helicopter skimmed over our roof, and we were informed through a booming megaphone that we would be airlifted to dry land. They began with people who needed medical attention, and Uncle Charles and Aunt Rose were among the first to be taken to safety. Then came the elderly people, and mothers with young children. The helicopter labored into the evening, and still the roof and the storage room were full of people. It wasn't until sometime on the third day that the city sent in a boat big enough to take the rest of us off that roof.

The boat took us as far as the St. Claude Bridge, from there to make our way on foot to find families and friends. I walked a few blocks to a public phone and called Mama's house to let them know I was all right. She told me that Uncle Charles and Aunt Rose had been taken to a hospital during the airlift but were now with her and that everyone was fine. Relieved and suddenly exhausted, I said I would be over as soon as I could.

There was a hot meal when I finally got there, and a hot bath. My sisters brought over some clothes for me. And the family gathered to offer up thanks for our having made it through the ordeal.

It seemed pretty clear that it would take us days if not weeks to get back to the house even to see how bad the damage was. Mama was living in a small apartment in public housing by this point, and there was no way she could put us up for any length of time. So we went to stay with Uncle Joe, my mother's brother, who was divorced by then and lived alone in a two-bedroom house. As I tried to get comfortable on the sofa in the living room the first night we were there, the thought occurred to me that I may not be going to college at all that fall.

Growing Up for Good

We finally got to look at the house about three weeks after the storm. Although we'd seen the flooding with our own eyes, I don't think any of us was prepared for how complete the devastation was. The water had risen all the way to the eaves of the house, and nothing could be salvaged. Everything we owned—our clothes, furniture, appliances—had been completely saturated by the stagnant floodwaters and had to be dumped. The house itself had to be gutted.

To make matters worse, we didn't know how we were going to pay for putting our lives back together. Flood insurance was not required back then, and the homeowners' insurance would only pay for damages from the tops of the windows up. The only way we could afford to repair the house and buy the things we needed to live was to take out a low-cost loan the government made available to people who had been affected by the hurricane.

The moment I saw that there was nothing left by the flood, I knew that I was not going to school that year. The fact that we would have to go into debt to rebuild only strengthened my resolve to get a full-time job, so I could contribute. The question was where to find a job.

Looking for a salaried position was very different from picking up summer jobs and part-time work on weekends. I was no longer a student earning some extra money; I needed to be an adult worker, bringing in enough pay to help support the family. Whatever anxiety I might have felt about this abrupt transition was pushed aside by the pressing needs of daily life. There was also relief in not having to pretend to be someone other than who I was: for the foreseeable future, I was a young adult doing what had to be done.

Through the grapevine, I heard that Southern Bell was hiring women to be telephone operators. I didn't even know that those kinds of jobs were available to African Americans and eagerly went downtown to fill out the application and have an interview. Right from the start, I was impressed by how welcoming everybody was. The white woman supervisor with whom I interviewed was very kind and polite. She congratulated me on graduating from such a good high school and complimented me on being well-spoken. When she showed me the switchboard room and the operators' lounge, I was surprised to see Black and white women working side-by-side. (There were no men, as I remember.) And I was happy to get warm greetings from many of them.

Best of all, I was offered a job as a local operator, starting immediately. All I knew about running a switchboard was the hilarious scene from *Auntie Mame* in which Rosalind Russell gets herself hopelessly tangled up as an operator at a large corporation. The reality, though much less entertaining, was more straightforward. I reported for work the next day and was given on-the-job training. We had a script and instructions for the basic procedures. A call came in, I answered, plugged the cable in the appropriate nest, dialed the number requested, and connected the parties. Except for the jokers who came out in droves on New Year's Eve and flooded the lines, I never had the same kind of trouble as poor Rosalind Russell.

From the start, the job at the phone company gave me a new sense of worth. I was proud to have gotten it in the first place, and I was pleased that I was doing well. Much more importantly, I was bringing home a paycheck big enough to help pay for our living expenses, to buy replacements for things we had lost in the flood, and to save.

When we got back to our house in late February of 1966

and life began to take on a more normal cast, I started thinking about what I could do to get myself into college. I saw people at the phone company who worked part time, and that gave me an idea. With the money I was saving, I would have tuition covered. If I got a regular part-time job on the switchboard, I could easily pay for books and living expenses and have enough left over to continue to contribute to the household.

Plan in place, I worked harder than ever for the next six months. My supervisors were as kind as ever when I talked with them and told them of my plan to attend college. They assured me that I would be able to switch to working part time five days a week. In September, I began attending classes at Southern.

Earning a Chance

That first year of college is a complete blur in my memory. I know that I took the core courses and did well in them. The rest of my freshman experience I recall as constantly trying to keep to a strictly regimented schedule.

In the morning, I took the bus to campus and went to class. Between classes, I studied in the library to keep up with assignments. Then in the late afternoon, it was back on the bus to go to the phone company. The one luxury I allowed myself was watching reruns of *The Twilight Zone*. We had a TV in the operators' lounge, and I made sure to get to work early enough each day to watch for a half hour while I ate supper. From six to ten in the evening, I worked my switchboard. The buses ran infrequently at night, so I rarely got home much before eleven. And the following morning, I started the whole thing over again.

Midway through the year, I started thinking: here I was

working my butt off, but I wasn't where I really wanted to be. Yes, I would be able to teach with a degree from Southern, but it wouldn't be the same as getting my degree from Dillard, the place I had dreamed of attending my whole life. In my mind, to have a real shot at joining the middle class, I needed to get a degree from an elite university like Dillard or Xavier.

Money, of course, remained a huge obstacle. Dillard's tuition was something like a thousand dollars a year then. To me, that might as well have been fifty thousand. But now that I was on campus, I learned that you could actually get a loan to go to college. Suddenly, my dream didn't seem out of reach.

Without telling anyone, I applied to Dillard for the following year and was accepted. I was also approved for a student loan that would cover my tuition, fees, and books. The rest I would continue to earn working at the phone company. Without even knowing it, I had gained a new kind of confidence that allowed me to take bigger risks. And the risks were paying off.

Dillard accepted the majority of my credits from Southern, and I started in the fall of 1967 as a sophomore. It was thrilling to walk through the familiar campus as a matriculated student. It was also terrifying.

My impostor fears kicked up big time from day one. The majority of my classmates, over seventy percent, lived on campus, even many city students. Very few worked. To me, it seemed like they were all in their natural element—they were entitled to be there—while I had to scrape and scratch just to get in the door.

I dealt with the feelings in the same way I had in the past: I kept my real life a secret, and worked really hard to put up a good front to appear to be just like everybody else. Yes, I was a city student. Yes, I worked part-time. But I didn't breathe a word to a soul about needing a loan to pay tuition, and I participated in campus life to the extent that I could. I made it a point to go to the student union on occasion, to be there for homecoming and other important events, to be part of the social life.

On the inside, I felt like an adult masquerading as a college kid. On the outside, I cultivated the persona of a serious, driven student who spent a lot of time in the library but also knew how to have fun when she chose to do so. So I might pal around with other kids in the dining hall, but when they brought out the cards and started playing Bid Whist, I would excuse myself and go to the library. To me, fooling around and playing games was a luxury I couldn't afford.

My studiousness brought on an unexpected blessing. Although I was still only a strong B+ student, that was enough to earn me a merit scholarship that paid for tuition and books. It was a gift from God for me. I did not have to go further into debt to continue my education, but more importantly the scholarship felt like much needed validation. It said to me, "You are smart and somebody is looking out for you and giving you a chance."

Without the extra financial pressure of the loan, I felt a little bit more at ease, and in my junior year even pledged a sorority—Alpha Kappa Alpha. I still couldn't do a lot because I worked every day, but being in the sorority helped me feel even more a part of life on campus. And off campus, Barbara and I, together with a few other college women I met through her, had organized a social club a few years earlier. We called ourselves the Aristocrats and began to organize balls in the old New Orleans tradition.

Of course, there was nothing unusual about a name like the Aristocrats. It was right in line with the grandiloquence of New Orleans social clubs. But in retrospect, for me, at least, the name did signify the aspiration to rise above my humble beginnings and to "make something of myself."

Crossing Class Boundaries

Racism and sexism were definitely the two big isms that shaped my experience as I was growing up. But it was the more subtle discomforts and pressures of navigating social class that often triggered impostor feelings during my college years.

Upward mobility is a central theme in the cultural narrative of our country. For African Americans and other historically disenfranchised groups it has been particularly important to move up in society as a way to redress the social, economic, and political injustice of the past. Yet the reality of upward mobility can be profoundly uncomfortable. Arriving at your destination, as I felt I had when I got to Dillard, can often feel like entering hostile territory, full of people who you fear are waiting to unmask you and brand you as a fake.

Rick Goings, the Chairman and CEO of Tupperware Brands, speaks very candidly about his own struggles with impostor feelings triggered by joining the social circles of wealthy people after having become a self-made success. Rick and I met in the mid-1980s, when he came to Avon. Rick impressed me with his business savvy, but even more so with his empathy and commitment to people. When after a number of years of tremendous success, he left Avon and took the top post at Tupperware Brands, I was elated. And I felt honored and excited when, a few years later, Rick asked me to join the company's board of directors.

Over the years, Rick and I have shared many stories and experiences and discovered our love for learning and a deep spirituality. We have learned a lot from each other.

Rick Goings: *A Skinny, Cross-Eyed Kid in a Ferrari*

My dad was a troubled soul. He quit school after the tenth grade to support his family, left home and became a radio announcer and musician. When the Second World War started, he went into the military. To enlist, he looked and looked for his birth certificate, but there was no record of an Everett Vernon Going. There was an Everett Vernon York with the same birthday as his. York was his mother's maiden name, so that's how he found out, at seventeen, that he was illegitimate. And he never did find out who his father was.

My parents met at the USO during the war and eventually got married. They settled in Chicago and had us kids. I have a sister who is a year older than I am, and another sister who is eight years younger than me. After he left the military, my dad worked for the Veterans Administration during the day and continued as a musician nights and weekends.

Our relationship was very volatile. Things got so bad between us by the time I was in high school that I had to leave home when I was seventeen. First, I lived with an aunt. Then, after a couple of months, I got my own apartment. I worked forty hours a week to pay my way, so finishing school was no easy feat. But I made it.

It helped that I had been used to working since I was really young. I had my first serious job at eleven. I had an ice cream bike, one of those freezers on wheels that you pedaled around. My mom still tells the story of how I came home after the first day all proud. "Mom," I said, "I made twelve dollars, and I had fun."

Then after that I was a caddy for two summers. It was a hard job, but really interesting. We had to carry two bags at a time. I was little, so that was a lot to lift. I got stronger, though, and I learned a lot. The most my dad ever made in his life was eight thousand dollars a year. This was a rich golf club, and I saw how people who had education and money talked and how they acted toward each other. Lights went on for me!

Next, I worked in a department store, where I scrubbed the floors and broke boxes down in the basement. I remember feeling like the Hunchback of Notre Dame. The door would open, light would shine in, and boxes would be thrown down to me, and I would break them up.

My self-esteem was pretty low when I graduated from high school. I was the second shortest kid in my high school graduating class. I had an eye that turned in, and I was really thin. So the way I saw myself was as a skinny little cross-eyed kid. Needless to say, I was not popular with girls.

After high school, I tried to sell encyclopedias for three months. Never sold a set. (Funny for a guy who is now running a big direct sales company.) Vietnam was beginning to bubble, so I joined the Navy.

The Navy was a huge transformation for me. I did well on the battery of tests they gave us, and so in boot camp they made me a platoon leader. Even physically, I started growing like mad; within two years, I was over six feet tall.

My self-image was changing. When I reported to my ship, I worked on the bridge as a quartermaster/navigator with the captain and the executive officer. I spent my time on watches talking to these guys who went to the Naval Academy, senior officers. And, you know, these were long hours out in the middle of the ocean and the Red Sea. I learned so much from these men, and I really looked up to them. I didn't hang around with the enlisted guys who were just chasing girls and getting drunk every chance they got. I said, "I am going to change my life."

I came out of the Navy as a petty officer and, more importantly, a different person, and I've never looked back. The G.I. Bill allowed me to go to college. I studied history at Guilford College, working forty hours a week in a men's clothing store. Senior year of college is when I started my first company, selling fire safety equipment with a friend of mine. I discovered that I was not a great salesman but a good recruiter, and the direct-sales company grew quickly. I quit school and devoted myself to the business full time.

Within a year, I split up with my partner, moved to Charlottesville, Virginia, and created a company called Dynamics, Inc., selling fire detectors. We used one-on-one direct selling, with a really creative approach. It was cool—a fun company. Then I franchised it. I never will forget getting the first check. I had sold a portion of St. Louis, and I remember lying in bed and saying, "When did God give me St. Louis?" I ran Dynamics for fifteen years and then sold it.

So I was in my twenties when I started making a lot of money. But I was living in Charlottesville, Virginia, and Charlottesville is a town of old wealth. I didn't have the kind of breeding that comes from growing up around horse farms and coming-out balls. I hadn't even finished college (a fact I hid carefully). All I had was a flashy car. There is a picture of me from that time wearing a cowboy hat and leaning on my Ferrari, the epitome of what members of the First Families of Virginia would disdainfully call "new money."

Although I became a member of a country club, I never felt fully accepted. I knew that people looked down on the business I was in. My then wife used to say to me, "Why didn't you go to law school? Why didn't you become a doctor?" She was from a very wealthy Kentucky family, and she'd tell people about what I did and apologize for me. Direct selling was considered a sleazy kind of a business. And having people look at me as just a slickster really triggered this sense that I was a fake, an impostor.

Fortunately, I found meditation around that time. It helped me, in the words of Ralph Waldo Emerson, to get my "bloated nothingness out of the way of the divine circuits." I settled into myself more, and my worries about being accepted subsided. And the next time they came up again, after I sold my company and joined Avon, I had a powerful new tool for managing the feelings. Yet after all the learning, the success, the adventures, I am still plagued by the impostor feelings from years ago.

Social status is a major source of impostor fears. But social status can be just so much "bloated nothingness." Money, whether old or new, is only as good as the use to which you put it. It is essential that you clarify your own values and look to build connections with people who share those values, regardless of their social class. Living an authentic life will help you minimize worries about not fitting in, no matter how high you move up the social ladder.

Chapter 4

Gender Matters

Get centered in yourself. We all have to contend with the fact that other people may make assumptions about us based on a whole host of markers we use to sort each other into categories, such as race, gender, age, religion, level of physical ability, sexual orientation, ethnicity, accent, class, weight, education, nationality, and so on. It is up to you whether you give power to these assumptions to trigger your self-doubt or work to remain rooted in your knowledge of yourself and your authentic self-confidence.

I was at work on the switchboard on April 4, 1968, when the evening news brought the tragic report of Dr. King's death. Even as we kept working, I could feel a current of anxiety, anger, and sadness pass among the women in the office. And it wasn't until I was waiting for the bus home at the end of my shift that I began to allow myself to become conscious of my own emotions.

I was suddenly very conscious of the fact that I was eagerly striving to take advantage of the opportunities that were opening up for African Americans thanks to the risks tens of thousands of people, including some of my classmates, were taking to demand equality. And I was painfully aware of the fact that I myself was only an observer in this struggle, feeling that I did not have the luxury of time to take part in these activities.

The whole ride home that evening, I carried on a debate with myself. On the one hand, there was the gnawing feeling that I was not doing my part to effect the changes I was benefiting from. On the other were the facts of my life: I had to study, and work, and help out at home.

This was an entirely new facet of feeling like an impostor. For the first time, I wasn't just worried about other people discovering that I was not the person I appeared to be, I wasn't quite sure I believed my own story.

But whether I believed the story or not, I had to carry on with my life. Next morning, after an uneasy night, I got up early as usual and went to class, then to the library to do my homework, to more classes, and then to the phone company for the evening shift. As I went through the familiar routine of the day, I slowly began to make peace with the fact that I had some degree of freedom to make choices in my life, but that my options were very limited. I simply did not feel I had the luxury of taking big risks that might jeopardize my finishing my education and getting a job, but I could do my part, even in a limited way.

What I was left with, though, was a new sense of yearning. I wished that I felt free to take that risk to get off the sidelines and really participate in the changes that were going on all around me.

Something to Prove

It took some time for that wish for something bigger to germinate. Through the rest of my sophomore year and all of junior year, I single-mindedly pursued the goal of preparing for a career as a math teacher. But in the summer of 1969, two seemingly small and unrelated events triggered a huge change in the way I looked at the world and led me to take a big risk that would shape the rest of my life.

Early in the summer, I went to a house party with my boyfriend, Robert. It was our first evening out together since he had come home after graduating from Boston University. There were many other new graduates at the party, and much of the animated talk was about people's plans for the future.

Robert and I fell into conversation with Ellis, a mutual friend who had just gotten his degree from Louisiana State University. Competitive and not one to mince words, Robert got right down to it. "So what are you doing with yourself, Ellis," he said, clearly eager to talk about his own plans.

"I am going to Columbia Business School, my friend," Ellis said proudly. "Got a fellowship and everything."

It turned out that Robert was also going to business school, at Harvard, which was news to me. So for the next fifteen minutes I listened to the two of them bragging about their test scores and fellowships and the kinds of plum jobs graduates of the respective schools got at major corporations. I had only the vaguest idea of what business school was all about, but from the conversation I got the definite impression that the prestigious universities were recruiting African American students to keep up with affirmative action. "Here is another sign of how things are changing for us," I thought and moved off to find someone more interesting to talk to.

It wasn't until a couple of months later into the summer that I discovered that the conversation about business school had struck a chord for me. I was out with Robert one Saturday night, and we got into an argument over some silly thing. But however it started, the argument flared up into a real fight about our relationship.

"You know what, Joyce," Robert glared at me, "you are just like all the other Black girls in this town. You're going to get your teacher's certificate, work for a couple of years, get married, and have a bunch of kids. And that'll be your life. You're never going to go anywhere or do anything."

He was an ambitious, driven young man, with a very high opinion of himself. Even though his mom raised him alone after his father passed away, he had enjoyed all the privileges of a middle-class upbringing. His mother was a teacher, and he went to a private Catholic high school and then to Boston University. In other words, he had exactly the kind of leg up in life that I felt I lacked. And here he was looking down his nose at me and telling me that I wasn't going to do anything he considered worthwhile with my life.

In the summer of 1969, feminism was a very remote concept for me. I was aware that the social change that was transforming the country included greater rights for women, but I had not started thinking about the role gender played in my own life. Yes, I was fully aware that there were only a few professions open to me as a woman—teacher, nurse, social worker; however, what I focused on was the fact that as an African American woman from a working-class family I could pursue a profession at all. Race and class put such huge limitations on opportunities that I honestly didn't stop to think about how gender contributed to these limitations.

But something about the way Robert had said "girls" felt like a slap in the face. My aspirations and my life, according to him, would be circumscribed by the fact that I am a woman. And all women's greatest ambition, according to this logic, is to marry and have children. In that instant, I fully experienced, for the first time, the corrosive power of sexism that claims that women do not deserve to be given opportunities because they do not really want them.

I was so angry, I could feel myself flush. "You can't define what my life is going to be like," was all I said, working hard to control my voice. The evening ended, and so did our relationship shortly after. But now I had something to prove, to myself as much as to anyone else.

In retrospect, I believe that I found Robert's comment so stinging because I recognized an element of truth in it. I was thinking about my future in a fairly narrow, traditional way. It wasn't true that all I was interested in was an "MRS" degree, but I certainly never even dreamed of doing anything more daring than teaching school. That was, in fact, the height of my aspirations up to that point. And suddenly I was asking myself why. Was I just settling for something safe because I was afraid to fail at something bolder?

I have learned over the years that for those of us who experience the impostor syndrome the idea of being seen as playing it safe is as great a threat as the fear of failing. And I don't know about you, but for me, there is nothing like getting good and angry to motivate me to take on a challenge. So I didn't dwell on what had kept me from dreaming big, I set out to prove Robert wrong.

Ivy League or Bust

I used what seemed like impeccable logic to formulate my plan. There appeared to be new opportunities for African Americans in business schools. Careers in business were prestigious. (I saw any job where you worked in an office as pretty highfalutin.) And business required good math skills. Ergo, I would apply to business school.

The only problem was that I didn't know the first thing about what was required. I had never even set foot in the business building at Dillard. Undeterred, I marched down there the first week of my senior year and was greatly relieved to find a wealth of information from several universities displayed on a table in the lobby. I picked up the packets from Columbia and Harvard, because those were the schools Ellis and Robert were attending. I also took one from the University of Chicago. (Just the previous spring, I had taken my first trip outside of Louisiana and my first airplane ride when I went to Chicago for the wedding of a friend who had dropped out of Dillard to get married. So since I had at least been to the city, Chicago was my third option.)

Lest people think I was crazy and try to talk me out of it, I did not tell a soul about what I was contemplating. As I have learned, one of the defining characteristics of those of us who experience the impostor syndrome is that we keep ambition and potential new successes secret until we are assured of the outcome, to guard against the possibility of public failure. So I pored over the materials in secret to figure out what I needed to do. It was a relief to learn that no undergraduate business courses were required and a real boost to see that there were fellowships available specifically for African American students.

I carved out time to prepare for the Graduate Management Admission Test and did well on the exam. I still didn't know whether I stood a chance of getting in, but I made up my mind and sent in my applications to the three schools.

Of course, I wasn't foolish enough to risk everything on this long shot, so I continued working diligently toward my degree in math education. And still I did not tell anyone about the new dream I was cultivating.

It turned out to be more than a dream; it was an attainable reality. Both Columbia and the University of Chicago accepted me, with offers of generous fellowships. (Harvard put me on the waiting list.) And now I really had to do some serious soul-searching. What was it I wanted to do with my life?

We were required to do practice teaching in preparation for getting a teacher's certificate. I was assigned to a middle school and taught seventh grade. They used to put us in at the end of the school day when the regular teachers were exhausted. So I taught a lot of fifth- and sixth-period classes.

Even though the kids were often a little restless and were not doing well in math, I found that I was able to engage them and to get them working. It helped that I was closer to their age and that I was coming in fresh. I threw myself into the teaching and challenged them. I was having fun doing it, and I think they sensed that and responded. So they tried harder, and their grades improved. That was really satisfying. I didn't delude myself into thinking that I had some special gift for teaching, but I was proud that I was able to help them achieve more.

So here I was, doing what I had been preparing for since high school, enjoying it, and succeeding. At the same time, I had not only an inkling of a much bigger world but a ticket to get there. But entering this new world required that I leave behind everything and everyone I knew and go off into entirely uncharted territory.

The prospect of leaving New Orleans and attending one of these "majority" institutions made me keenly aware of a deep-seated fear that I had not recognized up until then. I was afraid that I wouldn't be able to cut it in the mainstream. I was doing well in the environment I lived in—in segregated schools and a historically Black college. But I had absorbed—as I think most of my peers did—the often implied and sometimes overt message that the education we were getting was not equal to that of the white kids. So as I considered this great opportunity to drastically change my life, I was terrified that I was probably not equipped to succeed. I knew that either I would have to work like crazy to try and get by or I was going to fail.

Ultimately, I decided that this was my chance to take part in the changes that were going on all around me. Doors were beginning to open. I had been given an amazing opportunity, and I felt that I had to at least try it. The idea of the possibility was greater than the fear of failure.

Preparing to Fly

I made up my mind to go to business school and chose Columbia, because in addition to a fellowship that would cover the full tuition and books, the university had offered me a stipend for living expenses. For the first time since middle school, I would be able to concentrate entirely on my studies without having to worry about earning money too. I figured that I would need all the time and energy I could get to keep up in school.

The fear that I would fall flat on my face was strong enough that I made sure to have a solid back-up plan. I continued with my practice teaching and studied for the teaching certificate exam, which I would take in the summer. I had come this far down the road, and it didn't make any sense to quit now. If I flunked out of business school, or simply hated it, I would come back home and pick up where I had left off with the life I had planned for myself.

Through the entire last few months at Dillard and into the summer, I kept my new plans secret. After graduation, I stayed on part-time at the phone company and took a second job as an administrative assistant at a nursing home. In the meantime, I sat for the exam and got my teaching certificate. To my family and everyone around me, it looked for all the world like I was getting ready to start my career as a teacher in the fall.

It wasn't that I thought the family wouldn't be supportive, but the whole thing was so far outside their frame of reference. Where we lived, business was the neighborhood store and the department store downtown—and there weren't a lot of people who looked like me working down there still. So, the idea of a career in business was a foreign concept to my family. Teaching was a profession, not working in business. And you didn't need to go off to school in New York to do that.

The idea of my going so far from home, I knew, would be what the family would be most concerned about. As much as I hated to admit it, Robert was right. For the most part, folks from New Orleans—especially young women—stayed close to where they grew up.

So I kept my plans to myself until the middle of the summer. Barbara was the first person I told. Then, Robert, and later Ellis, who was going to be my lifeline at Columbia. And finally, my family. The opposition from the family came from a surprising source. It was Doris—who by this point was on her way to becoming an assistant principal—who was really set against my going away, because to her it was a scary idea. And she tried her best to get Aunt Rose to talk me out of it.

Aunt Rose and my mom were more perplexed than anything else. They couldn't understand what was driving me to give up everything I had worked for so hard and go off on this risky journey. In a way, that made it much harder, because I could not fully explain to them what this chance meant to me. So I played up the idea that I was leaving for only a short time and would be back home directly. Honestly, that's what I believed. I figured that I'd go, and if I did well, I would come back and get a job in one of the businesses downtown. I never thought that I would not return to New Orleans.

As these conversations stretched into August, I began to prepare to go in earnest. I had been saving money for months, in order to pay my way to New York, to have enough to fly home for vacation, and a bit of pocket money. I also needed to buy some new clothes that I felt would be appropriate for a big-city business school.

My major purchase was a suit. It was a kind of turquoise-blue, and I thought it was the cutest suit ever. I don't know how many times I thought I was going to wear it, but I was sure I needed it. It was my "image" suit. Other than that, it was just the necessities: slacks, skirts, blouses, and sundries. And of course, I had to buy a coat.

It was an exciting time. The weekend house parties that were—and still are—such a big part of the social life in New Orleans were buzzing with the energy of young people preparing to set off on the big adventures of their lives. This was our moment, and in one way or another we were all trying to make the most of the opportunities that were open to African Americans for the first time.

Facing the Big Isms

One of the big challenges that impostor feelings pose is that they can be triggered by a complex set of overlapping issues. For me growing up, being Black and from a family of very limited economic means created a sense of being underprepared. I was always worried about being a step behind the people I was competing with for opportunities. My being a female didn't play into these feelings, so it was not until I recognized that sexism would affect the kinds of opportunities I might have that I really became aware of gender discrimination.

For most women who entered the work world at the time when I did, struggling to have access to opportunities and having to prove their worth was a daily fact of life. My dear friend Anne Szostak, with whom I have the honor of serving on two corporate boards, has shared her very poignant story of fighting to feel worthy over the course of a thirty-year career in which she was one of a very small group of executives instrumental in growing a two-hundred-million-dollar local bank into a two-hundred-billion-dollar regional financial powerhouse.

Anne Szostak: *A Woman Worthy of Work*

I grew up in the bank that eventually became FleetBoston Financial—you might say I grew up with the bank. I started there as a management trainee in 1973, a couple of years out of college, when the bank was very small, with about two hundred million dollars in holdings. A sociology major, I landed in banking quite by accident. The department store where I worked after graduation had fallen on hard financial times, and I needed a new job. I bumped into one of my high school teachers and her husband, who was a trust officer, at a college alumni event. We got to talking, and he was kind enough to offer to introduce me to people at the bank. Before I knew it, I was a trainee.

I started out in human resources. That was really one of the very few areas open to women then. I did well and advanced. In about five or six years, I was promoted to assistant vice president, becoming the first woman to reach that level at the bank. That was the beginning of a string of many "firsts," as I moved up the ranks.

After I became a vice president, I moved over to operations, running all the backroom functions like bookkeeping and check processing. By 1983, I was senior vice president of retail banking, in charge of the bank's fifty branches, trust and private banking, mortgage and consumer lending, and MasterCard and Visa. And still, I was the most senior woman in management.

Throughout this time, I had to get used to being really tested. Running business areas where I was not the technical expert was hard. Often, I felt like I just didn't have a lot to add to the party. And people would test me because many of them were angry that someone like me, who hadn't grown up in their particular area, had gotten promoted. My being a woman certainly didn't help.

Fortunately, I had a boss who really helped me have the confidence to focus on leadership and management and also to trust my own instincts. Thanks to him, I learned that I needed to rely on my strengths. I am a good listener, and I can get disparate people to talk to each other to come up with solutions. I worked hard to piece things together and to understand the technical issues. Finally, the teams would come around and give me their trust and support.

I continued to advance, moving up to be executive vice president of consumer banking and then to corporate officer of human resources for the much larger company created by the historic merger of Fleet and Norstar. But even though I was the most senior woman in the company and part of the small group of officers who had contributed to the growth of the bank, I still felt like an outsider. Unlike my male colleagues, I wasn't promoted to be given a chance to live up to my potential. At every step, I felt I had to prove myself in order to advance.

The biggest test came in 1991 when I was named president of the Fleet Bank of Maine. Even the way in which I was promoted proved to be a challenge. The man who had the job was seriously ill, and there were conversations for months in the executive offices about who would replace him. I knew that my name was among those under consideration and was certainly eager for the opportunity. I was less than prepared for it when it came, though.

We were at home having dinner on a Thursday. The phone rang, and Mike, my husband, went to answer it. I continued chatting with our daughters, Brooke and Kate. Turned out it was my boss calling to tell me that I had been chosen for the job. "We want you in Maine on Monday," he said. "So clean up what you need to clean up in Providence and get yourself up there Monday."

It wasn't really an offer. I was told to upend my whole life in four days and get to work. The kicker came the following day when I found out that I was not getting a raise. My new boss told me that the senior management at the holding company decided that they'd rather have me just try it out for a while and had flatly refused his request for more money.

Even so, I did not feel like I had much of an option to turn down the job. Here was a historic opportunity. No woman had been a CEO of a bank in New England unless she had inherited it from her husband or father. To boot, I was not quite forty-one. So this was an enormous first—one I could not pass up.

Mike and the girls were supportive, although they weren't very happy about moving. For the first few months, I commuted, spending Monday through Thursday in Maine and coming home Friday night. Then the rest of the family moved up in June, when the school year was over. It was very stressful. Brooke had just finished seventh grade. Mike would have to drive down to Boston where he was covering the Celtics for his newspaper. And we would be away from my parents, who had always helped enormously with looking after the girls while we worked.

The job itself was really tough. This was during the financial crisis in New England. The bank was in very serious financial trouble; we had all these problem loans. And I was not a credit officer or a workout expert, so I felt very insecure about my ability to address the situation. The Federal Reserve regulators were all over us, and there was a lot of skepticism within the bank as to whether I could really do the job.

All of this was made much harder by the fact that I was the first woman in this role. Not only were there no role models but there was also all this added pressure to show that a woman could do it. Shortly after I got to Maine, I received a letter of congratulations from the entire staff of a bank branch. "We are so proud of what you are doing," it read. "We are all walking a little taller." The branch manager and all the tellers signed the letter. I was so moved, I welled up. And then I looked at the letterhead and realized that the letter was from a branch of one of our competitors.

My solution was to work harder than ever. I didn't want to let the bank or myself down. But I also didn't want to let other women down or let the bank think that a woman wasn't going to be able to succeed. And that was a pretty heavy load of pressure. I wouldn't wish that on anybody.

The solution had its limitations. I would get to work at five o'clock in the morning. Then by eight-thirty, I was so revved up, people who were just coming into work couldn't keep up with me. And after the third big crisis of the day, I couldn't really emotionally take on one more. So I learned to pace myself and to delegate.

I also remembered to work from my strengths. I wasn't a credit officer, but I have always been good with people. With the help of a consultant, I devised a strategy for dealing with the bank's bad loans. I got in the car and just drove up and down the Maine turnpike to visit all these companies and properties. Then, every Friday morning, the team would work on putting together workout strategies for each one. And after a few months, we started to make some progress.

When I started at the bank, we had a very bad rating of four on the Federal Reserve's rating scale. We set a goal of improving to a rating of one, which my team thought was totally impossible. In 1994, six months after I got transferred back to Providence to head up corporate human resources, we became a one-rated bank. There are very few banks in the country that are rated one. So, it was a very big deal. Despite my success in Maine, though, I was called back to headquarters, again with little option to choose.

Over the years, I have thought a lot about how I had been treated by the bank, and I was pretty angry about it. Although it was never spoken, it always felt to me as if the top executives were saying, "Okay, this is the game we're playing, and if you want to move up, you've got to prove that you can do it."

In hindsight, I might have had more leeway than I realized at the time. But it sure didn't feel like that, not when I had spent so many years as the only woman in the room. I finally realized what a burden all the "firsts" had been when I began thinking about leaving the bank in 2004. I felt like I'd done everything I needed to do, and I was ready to go, but I was still concerned about what that might mean for other women at the company and in the industry. Over dinner, I told a friend how I was feeling, and he said to me, "Why are you carrying all this for other women? They would want you to be happy. If they all knew how unhappy you are at the bank at this point, they would not ask you to keep going." I burst out crying, because finally all the weight of that responsibility had been acknowledged. It had been so hard, constantly trying to prove that a woman could do these jobs— constantly trying to prove that I was worthy of this work.

A common theme among the stories of people who suffer from the impostor syndrome is trying to alleviate the feelings of not being worthy by working harder and harder. Of course, there is a limit to just how much one person can work. And ultimately, it is never enough, since the external validation we are so eager for does not make the feelings that we do not really deserve it go away.

For women, there has been a particularly exquisite double bind. We have had to prove that we are worthy of work, but even as we have been doing that, we have had to contend with questions about our abilities as women in our social roles—as wives, mothers, daughters, friends, and coworkers. This has led too many women to try to be everything to everyone, except being themselves.

The way back from this fruitless and desperate pursuit is to ask what it means to you to be worthy in your own eyes. This is not an easy question to answer, but it is essential to ponder as you prepare to reclaim the joy, zest, and power of your life.

Chapter 5

What Color *Is* Your Parachute?

Get a reality check. Once you start looking at your impostor feelings, find a way to test whether your way of seeing yourself and your abilities and accomplishments is realistic. Ask yourself how you would view the same abilities and accomplishments in someone else.

Work on knowing yourself, on connecting with your calling, on leading an authentic life. You will still occasionally feel like an impostor, but the fear will be less intense and it will pass more quickly. Remember, it is your essence that defines who you are.

Memory is an odd thing. As I have thought back to coming to New York to attend Columbia Business School, I've discovered that I do not actually remember leaving home. I have no mental pictures of getting to the airport, or even boarding the plane. All I remember is my single-minded determination to get safely to my dorm.

The university had sent reams of information for new students, including detailed instructions for finding one's way to campus. I had been assigned a room in Johnson Hall, the women's dorm for graduate students. Originally intended to keep female students from distracting their male classmates, Johnson was on the east end of campus, right under the watchful eyes of the President's House. The building (which has been renamed Wien Hall) is located on 116th Street, between Amsterdam Avenue and Morningside Drive. The directions from the university emphasized that if you were taking a taxi from the airport, you had to make sure the driver dropped you off on the right end of 116th Street, to avoid Morningside Park, which separates Morningside Heights from Harlem.

The irony of the situation wasn't entirely lost on me. Here I was, a young African American woman on my way to matriculate at a majority institution for the first time in my life, and what I was told I had to be afraid of—and was, in fact, afraid of—was ending up in Harlem. All I knew of Harlem was what I had seen on TV, which was just enough to have it symbolize all the dangers of the big city for me.

Whether real or imagined, though, these dangers were knowable. What really terrified me was the alien new world that awaited me when I reached the "safety" of campus. I had grown up in a Black community, attended Black schools, and graduated from a historically Black university. Now, I was entering one of the most prestigious universities in the entire country, where African Americans still represented a tiny fraction of the student body and where I would have to compete with some of the best-educated young white men and women. The impostor feelings this brought on were overwhelming.

It was a huge relief when I finally checked in at the front desk of Johnson Hall and got up to my room. My roommate

Barbara, about whom I had read in the orientation packet, was already there. She was also an African American woman from the South just starting out in Columbia, so we had quite a lot in common, although she was attending the graduate program in the English department.

We had been assigned to a suite, with two bedrooms and a living space that we shared. It was very comfortable, and Barbara was nice and companionable. We chatted as I set up my room and then took a walk around campus and down to Riverside Park. It was Saturday, and lots of people were out strolling in the warm early evening. We weren't about to take any chances and only walked along the top of the park. The Hudson flowed fast and powerful, with boats heading upriver almost standing still in the current. The ornate buildings lining Riverside Drive looked majestic in the reflected sunlight. And the park itself gave off a cool scent of old trees and granite. I was intimidated and enchanted.

Among the Majority

The weeklong business school orientation began on Sunday. As nervous as I felt, I was also really excited to get started. Walking across campus that morning, I could finally believe that I was actually in graduate school—that I had made it. And I allowed myself to feel the thrill of the adventure.

The excitement served as a kind of emotional buffer as orientation began and I understood the degree to which I was in the minority in this world. Out of a class of approximately five hundred, there were only about twenty African Americans and only fifty or so women. It was one thing to know intellectually that there would be very few other people who looked like me, and quite another actually to see just how few.

It is not at all surprising that the Black students gravitated toward one another. By the end of that first day, I think, I had met most of the other African Americans in my class and had become friends with half a dozen of them, including Carolyn, Ernestine, and Mary, three of my closest lifelong friends. As the week progressed and we took part in the orientation activities, our group coalesced into a real community, one that gave shape not only to my time at Columbia but to much of my life since.

Funny enough, Johnie, the man whom I would marry many years later, was among the very last friends I met that first week. At the end of orientation, there was a beautiful reception at Faculty House for all the fellowship recipients. During the evening, someone introduced me to Johnie, a soft-spoken man with kind eyes and a musical Tennessee accent, and we started chatting. He had been teaching at Lane College and was at Columbia to get his MBA so he could move into administration. I told him about my degree in education and very limited classroom experience. He was easy to talk to, and since he was married, easy to be friends with.

As I had prepared to leave New Orleans, I had comforted myself with the thought that at least I would know one person in New York: Ellis, the friend who had been part of my inspiration for applying to business school. He was going to be my lifeline. But by the time Ellis came back for the start of classes for his second year of business school and my first year, I felt much less in need of a lifeline. Of course, it was great to have someone ahead of me to talk to about courses, professors, and so on.

Most of all, it was wonderful just to see a familiar face from home every once in a while.

It was that need to be among people with a shared experience that served as the glue for our group. We had grown up in a system that told us we were separate and unequal. And now that we were allowed to participate in one of its elite institutions, we clung to each other for the comfort of belonging. In essence, we segregated ourselves, functioning as our own social unit. This was a necessary defense mechanism against our collective anxiety. Although everyone started with a roster of core courses in the first semester, we were so few in that large incoming class that there were only one or two African American students in any particular section of a course.

I remember the panic I felt when I realized that I was the only Black student in my economics class. It was reputed to be among the hardest of the core, and the professor reinforced that idea when he announced on the first day that he was distributing the questions for the final exam right then and there because it would take us the entire semester to answer them.

"And I suggest you get in a team," the professor continued, "because you can't do this by yourself."

Talk about feeling like an impostor. It was one thing to be with all of these white students in class, where I could keep quiet and just do my best. It was quite another to work on a team with them, not able to hide how much I did or did not know. I was pretty confident in my math skills, though, and that helped. I took a deep breath and joined up with the four young men sitting around me. As it turned out, two of them were international students, so we made a very diverse team.

That first group project—one of many to come—was a critical step in my beginning to overcome the fear that my education had not prepared me to compete. Each of us took one of the five questions for the final and worked on it independently. We met a couple of times over the course of the semester and presented to each other. My work was every bit as good as that of my teammates, and I felt respected and equal.

Learning New Rules

The confidence I was gaining in economics was a much-needed antidote to my struggles with accounting. As most people not familiar with the subject do, I assumed that it was a mathematical discipline and that the same logic applied. Of course, nothing can be further from the truth. Accounting has its own rules. And I just didn't get it.

In other courses, when I had trouble, I just worked harder. But with accounting, working hard didn't get me anywhere, because I was missing the entire point. I would look at a balance sheet and try to get it to add up. The idea of just throwing in equity if it didn't seemed profoundly illogical to me. A formula either works or it doesn't. Why force it? What made the whole thing particularly confusing and painful was the fact that the instructor, who was the only African American professor in the business school, did little to provide any extra help.

As the semester progressed, it became clear that I was actually failing the course. I had never failed a class in my life and was despondent. And I didn't feel that I could get any support from the instructor.

The professor seemed to be making a point. Columbia had brought him on as part of its response to the student disturbances that kept flaring up after the protests that had shut down the university in the spring of 1968. Students were demanding greater representation of African Americans on the faculties of all the divisions, and the university was making strategic hires. I am sure that being the only African American on the faculty of the business school must have been difficult. And maybe the man felt he had to prove that he was not going to give any preferential treatment to Black students. Even so, that does not explain his seeming indifference to his students.

This experience with the accounting professor made me realize that there was a whole lot more to race dynamics than just which group you belong to. When I went back home for the Christmas holidays, I was keenly aware of how clearly defined and comfortable my world was in New Orleans. I am sure the feeling was that much stronger because of accounting. I hadn't officially flunked it, since we were to take our exams after the break, but I knew that it was a near certainty. Of course I didn't say it out loud, but in my mind I was preparing to pack it all in.

Fortunately, I was able to talk myself through the panic and the desire to flee. I used logic to calm myself, a technique that I would develop more fully later in life as a tool for dealing with impostor feelings. I thought about all the courses I was taking and had to admit that I was doing fairly well in all of them, with the notable exception of accounting. It seemed only reasonable that I should give myself the chance to take the exams and see how well I did.

That's how I got myself back to school. And yes, I did fail accounting. I admitted though that it might be a good thing that I had to take the class again, since I would probably need to know something about accounting to have a career in business. Therefore, I took it a second time and did begin to understand the accounting concepts and rules, earning a B in the class.

Finding My Footing

Most of my friends were interested in majoring in finance, but even though I was good with numbers, I wasn't drawn to that field. I am not sure I would have been able to articulate it at the time, but it lacked human interest for me. Marketing, on the other hand, which was among the core courses I took second semester, captivated me from day one.

Marketing was dynamic, not only allowing me to use my analytical skills but also tapping into creativity I was barely aware of. It gave me the opportunity to study people's motivations and decision making. Most importantly, marketing felt natural to me, a discipline in which I felt I belonged. For the first time in my life, I was doing something that did not require me to work extra hard just to keep up. I excelled without putting all that pressure on myself. Marketing felt right, and I just loved it.

When I had first decided to get an MBA, I had had no idea what I was going to do with it. A couple of months into that first marketing course, I felt as if a door had opened. I could see a path taking shape and a purpose and decided to pursue a concentration in marketing for my degree.

When I started taking courses for my concentration, I found myself the only Black student in class even more frequently than before. But somehow, that wasn't as important. In the marketing courses, I believed at my very core that I was good at what I was doing. I competed against my classmates with zest and determination. But the intensity was joyful rather than oppressive. I was having fun and did not worry about being an impostor. For the first time in my life, I believed in myself.

Race and Self-Doubt

Years later, when I first saw a copy of Dr. Beverly Tatum's brilliant 1997 book *Why Are All the Black Kids Sitting Together in the Cafeteria?*, my mind instantly conjured up the faces of my friends from Columbia. We were the Black kids huddled at a single table, painfully aware of just how different we were from everyone else around us. And that stark, inescapable difference was a constant trigger for the impostor fears: Am I here by mistake? Can I really make it? When will they decide I don't deserve this chance?

In her book, Dr. Tatum cites David Wellman's definition of racism as a "system of advantage based on race." Being one of only about twenty Black students (and that number declined after the first term) in a class of five hundred, it was hard not to feel that we were there through the goodwill of the majority group. We were being allowed to share in some of the advantages of the system. Seeing one's opportunities and accomplishments through such a lens, of course, raises all kinds of questions about your own merit and sense of agency. No matter how well-adjusted or confident you are, you cannot help but feel like an impostor.

Debra Lee, Chairman and CEO of BET Networks, is one

of the most accomplished women I know. She has been a dear friend for many years and served on the board of Girls Inc. when I led the organization. Among the many things I love and admire about Debi is how candid she is about the trials and tribulations she's encountered on her life's journey. Over the years, we've talked a lot about the challenges of often having been the only African American women in classes, meetings, and boardrooms. Debi's experience of, in the mid-1970s, going from the humanist campus of Brown University to the hard-driving atmosphere of Harvard Law School offers a particularly striking example of the powerful role race plays in triggering the impostor syndrome.

Debra Lee: *Discovering My Path*

My dad was a Major in the army, so we moved around a lot—Germany; Washington, DC; Los Angeles—until he finally retired and we moved to Greensboro, North Carolina, when I was in the sixth grade. One of the reasons we moved back to Greensboro was because my father was going to finish college at North Carolina A&T University. He wanted to be a lawyer like his sister, whom he really admired; she was the one of the first Black students to have gone to Mount Holyoke in the 1940s. Unfortunately, Dad didn't make it back to school, but he instilled in his kids the idea that you went to the best school possible. His dream for me was that I would go to an Ivy League university.

It was the middle of the 1960s, and Greensboro was a very segregated town. I went to an all-Black junior high and high school. That was a great experience because we had great teachers who were very dedicated. They taught us we could be anything we wanted to be. There was this expectation that if you were one of the good kids you were going to do everything right, perform well, and make your family proud, your community proud, your race proud.

When it was time to apply to college, I knew that I'd be going out of state. I had a cousin at Cornell. Dad thought I'd have a good chance at Yale, which had recently gone coed. And I had met some students from Brown at my high school and was really impressed with them. So those were the schools I applied to. I didn't get into Yale, and I didn't like Cornell when I went up for a visit. That's how I ended up going to Brown. And I loved it.

Going in, I don't think I had any fear about being able to compete. I had such good training from the teachers from my high school and had such confidence, I wasn't afraid that I couldn't do as well as the white students. And once I got there, I found students who looked like me, who were from backgrounds similar to mine. There was a big enough population of Black students that I felt comfortable.

Intellectually, I felt challenged and excited. Brown had a new curriculum that allowed you to make up your own concentration. I majored in Chinese communist ideology—because it was the 1970s. I actually went overseas my junior year. I couldn't get to China, because the country was still closed to Americans at the time, but I went to Thailand, Malaysia, and Singapore in 1975, right as the Vietnam War was ending. That was quite something.

I did really well at Brown. I met good friends and became active in organizations; after my first year, I became a peer counselor, advising freshmen. I just had a really great positive college experience.

As I got closer to graduating, I started thinking about what I was going to do next. My dad also always wanted me to be a lawyer, so I always had in the back of my mind that I might go to law school. I was really never that excited about it, but after four years of majoring in Chinese communist ideology and political science, I figured I was going to law school. I respected Thurgood Marshall and what lawyers had done during the civil rights movement, and I thought law would be a great way to contribute to social change.

My boyfriend from Brown had gone to UCLA Law School, so I had it in my mind that I would go to school in California to be near him. When I went to talk to my dean about my plans, I told him I was applying to Stanford, Berkeley, and UCLA. I also threw in Georgetown and Columbia, just to make it look good. "Well," he said, "you know you have a really great record. You should really apply to Harvard or Yale." When I objected because I wanted to study in California, he persisted, telling me that I owed it to myself to try for these two top schools.

Since Yale had rejected me for undergrad, I wouldn't hear of applying there, but I compromised and agreed to apply to Harvard. I left his office in tears, because I knew that if I applied and I got in, I would have to go. That's just the way I was raised: you go to the best school you get into.

I didn't even tell my father that I had applied to Harvard, because I wanted to make my own decision. And sure enough I got in, and sure enough I felt that I had no choice but to go.

That's when the impostor syndrome showed up big time. I had a white friend whom I had met sophomore year. We lived next door to each other in double rooms that shared a bathroom. And the four of us—she and her roommate and I and my roommate—all became fairly good friends. This young woman applied to law school at the same time I did. When she learned that I had gotten into Harvard, where she had been rejected, she said jokingly that I had gotten in because I was an affirmative action case.

And having a friend say that really stuck with me. Harvard is Harvard, and supposedly only the best and brightest go there. I had gone to Brown without a lot of self-doubt, but when I got to Harvard, I was suddenly anxious. I was worried that maybe I didn't really belong. I was sure that at some point someone was going to discover that I was a mistake. I wasn't going to be successful and would let my family down, and my community down, and my race down—all the people who were depending on me because I had done this wonderful thing of getting into Harvard.

The environment at the school did nothing to allay my fears. Unlike at Brown, there were not many people like me, or from a similar background, or with whom I really had a lot in common. I had one good friend who was from Alabama, but she was in another section, so we couldn't even really help each other with coursework. I never joined study groups, because I was afraid I wouldn't be accepted. I didn't even socialize with my classmates, instead spending more time with friends from the medical school, so I could get away from the law school.

Most professors were happy to ignore the Black students and the women. We had classes with 140 students, and the people who always raised their hands and were called on were very different from me. There were usually no minorities and no women. And the professors, with very rare exceptions, just looked past us. The message seemed to be, "I don't expect you to do well, and I'm not going to call on you."

That first year, I ended up hating law school, which I kind of figured I would. I felt very alienated, and I wasn't even learning the kind of law I thought I might want to practice. But I knew I couldn't waste this opportunity and just drop out. So, I applied to the Kennedy School of Government and got in for the joint program, which meant

I did one year of law school, one year at the Kennedy School, and then two years at both, finishing with a JD and a master's in public policy.

Even with all the heartache of the first year, I had done well enough to know that I could do the work. And once at the Kennedy School, I felt I could relax and figure out what I wanted to do. I was out of the traditional law school track and didn't feel the pressure to compete with my classmates or do what they were doing. On my own path again, I did really well in my studies and no longer felt like an impostor.

Race is a powerful trigger for impostor feelings. Whether consciously or not, people often make assumptions about others based on the color of their skin. The important thing for each of us to come to terms with is how to be in relation to the assumptions people may make about us.

Debi's story of losing her emotional balance in law school and then regaining it when she found a more authentic path is a vivid illustration of how impostor fears based on race can materialize when we lose connection with ourselves. At those times, it is no longer other people's assumptions we have to grapple with but our own.

For me, it was all too easy to believe that I was not prepared for an Ivy League business school when I didn't know why I was there. When I discovered marketing, I didn't magically become better prepared. I now had a purpose that allowed me to feel I belonged. And with that, I did not worry nearly as much about any assumptions anyone else was making about me.

Chapter 6

But You Are So Young

The terrible irony of the impostor syndrome is that it shows up most intensely to make us question whether we are worthy of our accomplishments at the very moment we succeed. And since it is a form of social anxiety, it forces us to compare ourselves to our new peer group—to people who have succeeded in a similar sphere—and to worry about the ways in which we do and don't fit in. Most often, we focus on the nonnegotiable aspects of ourselves, those things we cannot change.

Analyze your success. Our impostor fears tell us that our success is, at worst, a fluke and, at best, the result of extraordinarily hard work. Develop a written inventory of your skills, accomplishments, and experiences to build an understanding of your success and to begin to exercise your skills of internal validation.

Since I had made the decision not to work during school, I felt that I needed to graduate as quickly as possible and start a career. It seemed to me that I simply did not have the luxury of taking the full two years to get my degree. I took classes pretty much nonstop for a year and a half and graduated in February of 1972.

My plan, it turned out, didn't take into account a couple of factors that made getting a job a real challenge. The U.S. economy, while still growing quickly, was heading toward a historic reversal. A *Time* cover story in March, 1972, asked "Is the U.S. Going Broke?"

Closer to home, and more important for my prospects of finding a job, was the fact that most corporate recruiters only came to campus in May, when the majority of students graduated. So I was only able to get two or three interviews that winter. I was discouraged not only by how few opportunities I had but also by the sense I got from the interviews of the kinds of challenges I was likely to face once I did get a job in corporate America.

An interview I had at that time with a recruiter from the Scott Paper Company was particularly striking. We had had a good conversation and were wrapping up. The man paused and said to me, "You know, we don't have any women in our marketing department."

I was incredulous. Here was a company whose consumers were 99.9 percent female, and they didn't have any women doing marketing. It was a real reminder of just how huge a cultural shift I was taking part in.

When February rolled around, I had my brand-new diploma but no job. I didn't entertain any thoughts of packing up and going home, because I couldn't think of how to do marketing in New Orleans. In my mind, I needed to be in New York, or somewhere like it, to be able to do this thing I had discovered was my calling. After a couple of months of frustration and anxiety, I learned through the placement office at Columbia that the City University of New York was recruiting MBAs to come in and help run the business side of its large system. At that point, I needed a job, any job. So even though this was not a position in marketing, I went to interview and got a position in the business office.

I was so excited. My starting salary was $13,500, and I thought I had hit the jackpot. By this point it was May, and both Mary (who like Johnie was enrolled in the dual MBA/ EdD program) and Ernestine were graduating. The three of us decided to room together and got an apartment at 733 Amsterdam Avenue, one of those newer apartment complexes on what was then a grittier section of Manhattan's Upper West Side.

You Are Not What We Expected

At City University, I was assigned an interesting project. The university was the controlling agency for the twenty city colleges, which included the community colleges and four-year schools. Up until then, City had never evaluated the colleges from a business perspective. And now they wanted to look at them as profit centers, to see which ones were doing well, which were the most profitable, and so on.

The work took six months, but the findings were really interesting. It was clear that many of the colleges had particular strengths. For instance, Hunter had an outstanding program in education, and Baruch one in business. Yet each college offered courses in all the disciplines. It just wasn't efficient.

In my report to the vice chancellor, I made a bold

recommendation. It was evident that from a business standpoint the system was not productive. I proposed, therefore, discontinuing classes that were outside each college's area of concentration and having students take them at sister institutions. So, for instance, a Hunter student interested in a business class would take it at Baruch, and a Baruch student interested in an education course would take it at Hunter.

This apparently was not what the university wanted to hear. They appeared to think that this was just the naïve perspective of someone young. "Okay, that's nice," they told me, "but this is not what we were looking for." And they hired McKinsey & Company to come in and do the study again.

I was relegated to a corner of the business office responsible for making modifications to budgets as they came in from the colleges. It really didn't take a whole lot of intellectual capital to do this, and it didn't take a lot of time. To keep myself busy, I learned as much as I could about the benefit plan and taught people about their packages. I had to keep working, since I had to eat, but I decided that there was no way I was staying in that job.

As I pored over the "Help Wanted" ads in the evenings and wrote my cover letters, I thought about my experience at the university and realized that there was yet another defining characteristic that might present challenges in my career. I had recognized that being from a working-class family and being African American might present obstacles. I had also learned to recognize that being a woman might pose some challenges. Now, I was beginning to see that my being young might also keep people from recognizing my skills and contributions.

Trailblazing Is Just another Word for Bushwhacking

I had a job and therefore the luxury of being strategic about my job search. Unlike the frenzied way I sent out resumes at the end of my time at Columbia, I now concentrated on opportunities that would actually start me on a career path in marketing. Two companies that were recruiting seemed particularly interesting to me: Avon and Columbia Records. I interviewed at both and found myself really drawn to Avon. I liked the company, and I liked the position they offered me.

So in early 1973, I joined Avon's merchandising department as an assistant planner. This was an entry-level position in the unit that was responsible for creating campaigns or marketing plans for the company's two-week sales cycles. It was a great way to learn the business. In creating a campaign, you used the entire Avon product line to achieve the dollar and profitability goals for each cycle. The creative part was developing a promotional theme and putting the product together to support the concept. Then you had to set the right pricing to meet the goals for that two-week period. For me, the work offered an exciting way to combine my math background with what I had learned in business school.

Of course, I was nervous as anything going in. I saw the job in the same way I had seen being accepted to Columbia— an opportunity I was being given—and I was anxious to prove that I was worthy of that opportunity. Secretly, I was terrified that I would be found lacking in preparation, intellect, and ability.

The impostor fears started creeping up on me even as I interviewed for the job. With the exception of a woman in human resources, every other person I met with was a man. When I started at the company, I was only one of four women in the merchandising department; two had been there for about a year, and one started at the same time as I did. On the product marketing side, there were also four women, and none of us was in a position more senior than planner.

In the entire company, there were very few women in executive jobs. A major breakthrough came about a year after I joined Avon when the first two women were promoted to vice president, one in marketing and one in sales. It was remarkable that, up to that point, this enterprise built on the idea of women selling products to other women had not had a woman in a leadership position.

I was even more keenly aware of how few other African Americans there were in the company. Just as I had been in business school, in those early years at Avon I was usually the only Black person in the room—particularly in marketing meetings. Avon was, however, among the corporate leaders in addressing the need for diversity, or what at the time the company called "multiculturalism." It had written principles and was working to implement them. A year or so before I joined, a group of employees had organized a Women & Minorities Committee, which was then officially sanctioned and advised the president on the concerns of these two groups through regular meetings.

In 1973, however, the fact of the matter was that white men were running the show. It was their world, and they shaped the policies, set the style, and made the rules. We were pioneers in this world, and even though we had been invited in, it was hard not to feel like an interloper. We did not know how to act or how to dress. With no role models, the only option, it seemed, was to try to fit in by trying to be like the men who ran the company.

To me it felt like yet again I was on my own, attempting to succeed in an alien environment, with no elders to guide me. And with that came the familiar questions: What makes me think I can do this? What happens if I can't? How long until someone finds out that I don't really belong here?

Fortunately, Avon was a nurturing environment, dedicated to helping people succeed and to promoting from within. I got lots of positive reinforcement and opportunities to learn and grow. I got a real boost when I was promoted from assistant planner to associate planner within my first year at Avon. It was tangible validation that I was doing the right things and succeeding. But the impostor syndrome doesn't allow any success to go unpunished. Within a week of the promotion, I was worrying about being able to perform at this higher level of responsibility. And I worked even harder to prove that I could do the job.

That pattern repeated itself with unfailing regularity over the next few years. I worked hard and was rewarded with a promotion every twelve to eighteen months. And with every promotion, the impostor fears drove me to work that much harder to show I deserved it.

What I began to notice was that the fear not only made me work crazy hours but also kept me from seizing opportunities to shine. In meetings with senior executives, I found myself passing up chances to speak up and share my ideas. I was so concerned about saying something wrong and looking dumb that I simply clammed up. What galled me most was that just as often as not, one of the guys would say exactly what I had been thinking. After that had happened a few times, I had to admit that I was just standing in my own way and tried to convince myself that I had earned my place in those meetings. It took some time, but gradually I began to speak up.

I thought back to an experience I had at the end of my time at Columbia. The last of the core courses was one you couldn't take until the last semester of your second year. It just so happened that Mary, Johnie, and I were all in the same section. (Mary and Johnie finished their business school coursework at the same time I did, although they continued through May to complete the EdD courses.) But although there were three of us, we were still pretty intimidated by how different we were from the vast majority of the students in the class. Throughout the semester, we kind of huddled up at the very top of the lecture hall and did not utter a word.

This being business school, there was a final group project to analyze a company. The three of us formed a team and decided that we were just going to go for it. We didn't come out and say it, but we all knew that this was our chance to show that we deserved to be there.

We studied the company we had chosen from every angle possible: finance, organizational behavior, marketing, you name it. We had graphs and charts and diagrams. Johnie, who has always been a really good typist, typed up the paper, and we all rehearsed our oral presentation for days.

On the day we were to present, we showed up in class dressed to the nines, in our best business attire. Our turn came, and when we finished presenting there was total silence in the hall. Everybody—the professor and all the other students—just looked at us for a few moments in complete surprise.

And then the professor actually said, "That was one impressive presentation. Where have you all been this whole term?"

I returned to that moment many times as I encountered my fears about being less prepared or less intelligent than others. I used the story to remind myself that when I stayed silent all I gave people was a blank canvas on which to project their own preconceptions of my abilities. More importantly, I pushed myself to remember that I had valuable things to contribute.

Girls in a Man's World

Avon was a youthful company. Even at the director and vice president levels, most people looked quite young. So my age wasn't among the factors that triggered the impostor syndrome in those first few years. When I became a manager, however, I notice that I was comparing myself to more senior people and wondering whether I measured up.

I first became aware of it in a kind of humorous situation after I took over as the manager of merchandising of the Canadian business. I was based in New York, along with the planners who now reported to me, and traveled back and forth to Montreal, where the operation was located. On my first trip there, I came into the office and met everyone. After we had made the rounds, the regional director and I sat down over a cup of coffee to get acquainted.

"And how are things in New York?" the man said in the kind of way you ask about the weather. "How are Pat's girls?"

He caught himself and looked at a loss for words. Pat was the man who had managed the group before me, and the planners, who were all women, were apparently known as "Pat's girls."

"I mean, the women...," my colleague said, trying to regain his composure, "... the ladies in the department."

I did not take offense. I was the first woman to have become a manager in merchandising in Avon's Canadian business, so it would take everyone a bit of time to adjust. That word "girls," though, did stick with me. It seemed to carry with it an implied dismissal, a suggestion that the women were not to be taken seriously. I didn't spend a lot of time on linguistic analysis, but it was clear to me that the word was another not-so-subtle reminder of who held the power.

I was reminded of this episode in 2010, when I delivered a keynote speech at the Dr. Martin Luther King, Jr. Day Celebration at Miss Porter's School for Girls. On arrival, I was impressed by the young, energetic head of school, Katherine Gladstone Windsor, and after my speech, she and I fell into a long, fascinating exchange about what we were learning from the girls we worked with. Kate shared with me the findings of the research she had conducted for her Ph.D dissertation that showed that girls see men, rather than women, as successful, because, as a group, men still control money and power. And I told her about a Girls Inc. study in which girls expressed their worries about their inability to meet the growing social expectation that they excel at everything and still please everyone.

That, in turn, led me to mention the impostor syndrome. Kate, who was very familiar with the term, paused, seemingly deciding whether to share a confidence, and then told me of her own struggles with the fear that she was unfit for leadership. She had become successful very early in her career, and for her the doubts repeatedly centered on whether she was too young to serve rightfully in her successive posts.

"It is reasonable to be fearful—to feel uncertain to some extent—when you are doing something for the first time," she said thoughtfully, "but it can get to the point of becoming paralyzed. Who you are and how you are, those things that are nonnegotiable about you, affect how you see yourself as a leader and how people experience you as a leader. The fact is that women and people of color—and younger women and people of color in particular—face significant hurdles in being accepted as leaders."

Kate's experience with success at a young age and her research with girls offer essential insights into the ways in which our cultural and sociopolitical environments shape the triggers for the impostor syndrome.

Katherine Windsor: *What Does It Take to Feel Successful?*

In my doctoral research, I wanted to understand better how young women think about success, since that informs how they experience it. To feel successful, you have to know what your goal is and what you think is going to happen when you reach it. Part of the impostor syndrome, I believe, is a disparity between what drives people to achieve and the reality of success.

For young women, in particular, there is a real gap between what we encourage them to believe and how things are in the world. We are now two generations into the women's movement, and the options that are available to girls are vastly expanded. We tell them that they can do anything. So people go into their careers and chase their ambitions with the expectation that this is true. But, in fact, the sociopolitical domain is very different, and there are very few women who enjoy the privilege of having power and authority and who receive top salaries. This feeds a sense of uncertainty about whether or not you really have arrived or whether you have what it takes to be successful.

Recognizing yourself as part of an underclass in the context of a dominant culture is what, I think, sets off the impostor syndrome. And cultural dominance can take on many forms and can assert itself in a variety of ways.

If you look at me from the outside, I am a white, straight, Christian, married woman who was raised in a background of privilege. I have a successful career and a fulfilling family life. And yet, I have struggled with impostor feelings in a profound way.

I grew up in a highly educated Quaker family in Baltimore. Both my parents were educators: my father was a school superintendent and my mother a principal. I have always been really driven and was very successful in school. I did well academically, was president of my high school class, and was a star athlete. My parents expected great things from me, and were surprised when I decided to go into education after college, leaving me wondering whether I was doing something important enough with my life.

In my first job, I was hired to coach lacrosse at a boarding school. And even though my degree was in English, I was assigned to the all-male history department. At the first departmental faculty meeting, when I was introduced, one of my new colleagues said loudly, "My goodness, I have sweaters older than you." So that was my introduction to teaching, and it only got harder when I was named a department chair a relatively short time after. I started dreading telling people what I did, because I constantly had to answer the question, "How did you get that job?" In fact, that question has haunted me my whole career.

I became the head of school at an independent school in Boston at the age of thirty. At the time, I was the youngest woman leading an independent school. This was so unheard of that a group of parents challenged my appointment, alleging that I had not been properly vetted. Ten years later, when I left the school to take my post at Miss Porter's, they named the arts and athletic wing after me.

I am now in my mid-forties and have been head of school for nearly fifteen years, and yet at professional conferences when I introduce myself I still get the same response. Some people don't register my title and sometime during the conversation ask, "And what do you do at Miss Porter's?" Others look surprised and say things like, "How old are you?" or "Do you have children?" or "How did you get the job?"

"Well, I applied," I usually want to say, but of course I know what they are asking. And it still makes me feel anxious.

What I found stunning in my research is that girls have watched the women of my generation go through our struggles and they are drawing their own conclusions. And they are pushing back. One girl said to me, "You know, you are really good at telling me how to be a Supreme Court Justice. You line that up for me. I know how to go to school, what internships I need, and so on. But that has nothing with to do with living my life."

We say over and over, "You can do anything and be anybody you want to be." But they look at the experiences that their mothers have had and those of women in positions of leadership and power, and they don't buy it. They don't buy this idea that if you work hard, and you go to the right college, and you get the right internship, and you pay your dues, you are going to have a successful and fulfilling life.

Even when I talk to them about finding a life for themselves that's fulfilling and purposeful, they feel that it's harder than ever.

Their mothers' and grandmothers' generations could at least talk about what the issues were. Now they are expected to have this façade of everything being perfect, particularly if they follow a specific high-profile trajectory. Success is still being defined by the dominant culture, and that sets up powerful internal conflicts for the individual.

Success at a young age can be very disorienting. On the one hand, it is wonderful to have the validation of being entrusted with responsibility and authority. On the other hand, early success often leads people to question their own skills and maturity. Impostor fears rise up and make us wonder whether we are actually experienced enough to handle the responsibility. At heart, this fear is about being rejected as an uppity kid trying to pose as an adult.

People who experience the impostor syndrome are, on the whole, very driven and ambitious. You succeed not just because you work hard but also because you have the ability to do the job. That's difficult to remember, though, when that hard work gets you to the next level of achievement and the fears rise up.

Chapter 7

Climbing the Ladder

The biggest challenge the impostor syndrome poses for those of us who experience it is that it is impossible ever to work hard enough to quell the feeling of not belonging. Our fear tells us that if we put in the extra hours, prepare better, and sacrifice more, we will have earned our place at the table. The same fear, however, constantly reminds us that we are from the wrong side of the tracks, that we don't look like everyone else, that we are not as smart, and so on and on.

Question your work habits. If you are like most people who experience impostor fears, you are likely to compensate for feeling unworthy by working harder than anyone else around you. Stop for a moment and ask yourself whether the hard work is making you feel less like a fake. Then, begin to consider what makes you feel truly worthy in your own eyes.

There is now widespread debate about the origin of the notion of the "glass ceiling." The term came into popular use after it appeared in a 1986 *Wall Street Journal* story about the barriers to advancement women executives encountered in the corporate world. In the 1970s, the few women and people of color who were moving into the ranks of middle management didn't necessarily have language to describe what we were experiencing but knew that there were real challenges to getting ahead.

At Avon, the Women & Minorities Committee worked to bring these issues to the attention of senior management and to find ways to address them. The company embraced this effort and invested in understanding and building diversity. After I had been with Avon for about three years and had been promoted as many times, management asked me to join the Committee. I took this as a big compliment and as another sign that I was viewed as a real contributor, someone with a future in the company.

As a member of the committee, I had an intimate view of the enormous effort that was required to begin to change the culture. Avon started doing a lot of diversity training to try and get people to understand the inherent biases that everybody carries. It seems rudimentary now, but at the time we were all learning about the potential red flag of bias when someone says something like, "I don't have problems with Black people. Some of my best friends are Black."

I remember one training session in particular. There was a sizable group of middle managers. The facilitators put up flip charts around the room, each one with the beginning of a sentence: "Blacks are...", "Hispanics are...", "Women are...". They invited us to complete the sentences. "Don't screen anything out," they said. "Just throw out everything that comes to mind immediately. Things that you've heard, you felt, you think." And it was a shocker. Once people got going, they spewed out some of the most prejudiced things you can imagine. It's one thing to have a general sense that people have biases. It's quite another to see these biases, even your own, written down on paper.

For me, this was very disconcerting because I had had such a positive experience at the company. All my managers had been very supportive and had given me every opportunity to succeed and advance. Some of the things I heard, though, gave me real pause, and I worried that some of these biases would present insurmountable obstacles to me as I tried to build my career. However, it was also necessary preparation for the moment when I did inevitably encounter the glass ceiling.

When I did, it felt like I had run into a concrete wall. The shift from feeling successful to having my every move questioned was that sudden. It happened when I was promoted to manager of merchandising of the Canadian business. This was a big step for me, and I was super excited—especially so because I was offered the job by Jack Lausten, a marketing executive who had taken a real interest in my work and become a kind of informal mentor. Unfortunately, about a month after I started in my new role, Jack left the Canadian business when he was promoted to vice president of one of the product marketing departments, and I had to report to a new director (oddly enough also named Jack).

Well, as far as this Jack was concerned, it seemed I couldn't do anything right. It felt like my worst fears coming true. I was working harder than ever, and yet I kept getting the message from my boss that I wasn't doing that good a job.

What made it worse was the fact that the culture at Avon was very nonconfrontational, so it was hard to get direct feedback. My own fears got in the way of asking for feedback. I was too afraid to hear that I just wasn't doing very well. I got my annual review, and that was all the feedback I could handle.

So when things weren't going well with my boss on the Canadian business, there was just this constant churn of anxiety, but I didn't know what wasn't working. And I didn't know what to do.

The situation came to a head after one particularly disturbing conversation. "You know, Joyce," my boss said to me in one of our regular meetings, "you're so good with people, I think maybe you should be in human resources." To me, that felt like a slap in the face. He wasn't saying I had great human resources skills, but rather that he didn't think I was very good at my job. In addition, I had always been in a line position, and that is where I wanted to stay.

For women, at that time, having profit and loss responsibility was very significant, and I wasn't prepared to give up what I'd worked so hard to get. I hadn't taken all the risks up to that point only to be pushed out of the real competition. "Well, actually, Jack," I said, trying not to show just how angry I was, "what I'd really like is to get back on the U.S. business."

The conversation made it clear, though, that this man was likely to stifle my career. I knew I had to do something, and I went to talk to Jack Lausten. He was now fully established in his role as vice president of product marketing and was very highly regarded in the company. And I knew that he had my best interests at heart. Jack listened attentively, as he always did, told me not to do anything rash, and said he would see how he could help.

True to his word, Jack found a manager position for me in his organization within a few months. He even had the good grace to allow my director to take the credit for putting my name forward for the job.

By this point, I had been at Avon for nearly five years. I had advanced quickly, but the experience of having a boss who was less than supportive made me wonder whether the honeymoon was over. The next step up would be a director position, and I suddenly wasn't sure how accessible it would be for me.

I also started thinking about my career in general. In the personal care industry, at that point, people looked at Avon only as a direct-selling company. At places like Revlon and Lauder, folks didn't really think of us as marketers. In their eyes, since we were using a direct-sales channel, we weren't really doing marketing, just promotions and sales. I began to worry that if I stayed with the company too much longer, I would be pigeonholed in this way, which would severely limit my options.

Culture Shock

As it often happens, when you open yourself up to opportunities they present themselves. A friend at Avon recommended me to a headhunter who was recruiting marketing people for Revlon. When we spoke, the recruiter explained that the company was restructuring its marketing organization and bringing on a handful of new marketing directors in the process. I went for several rounds of interviews and was offered the position of Director of Marketing on the Polished Ambers brand, the company's new line of beauty products for African American women.

This was a fantastic opportunity. It was a high-profile new brand in a category that the large beauty companies were just beginning to enter, and I would be going in as a director. If there was ever a way to test my abilities as a marketer, this was it.

Of course, there would be a price to pay. Although Charles Revson, Revlon's founder and longtime manager, had died in 1975, his spirit and tough-minded way of doing business still permeated the company. To find out what it was like working at Revlon, I called a former Avon colleague who had gotten a job there a year or so earlier. I told her about the offer, and before I even got a chance to ask her any questions, she said, "Joyce, if you're going to come here and work for that woman, don't come."

I was really taken aback. I had met with the vice president to whom I would report and the group vice president to whom she reported. Both women were very professional and quite personable. Annette Golden, the group vice president, was particularly impressive, and I knew that I would learn a lot from her. But it really gave me pause to have someone who knew the cultures of both companies give such a dire warning about my prospective boss.

Ultimately, I decided that this was very much like the opportunity to go to business school. It was a big gamble, but if I succeeded, I would be playing at a whole new level. And that seemed like a worthwhile risk.

As I have been thinking about the impostor syndrome, I have come to see that it had driven me to take on tougher and tougher challenges. Getting to a comfortable place and staying there was never an option, because settling for comfort in itself seemed like a failure. I knew I would be walking into a really tough environment at Revlon. And now the challenge was to prove that I was tough enough to withstand it and succeed.

As it turned out, the culture was even more intense than I had expected. I will never forget the welcome reception for new employees the company hosted about a month after I started. It was very elegant, with beautiful flower arrangements and wonderful food. Annette, the group vice president who so impressed me when I interviewed with her, gave a welcome speech. "We're trying to do new things at the company," she said. "And we're so happy to have you."

But then the president of the company came in to give his speech. He had grown up in that "chew-'em-up-and-spit-'em-out" culture, and he did not mince words. "Take a good look around," he said, "because you won't see half these people in a year. Most of you won't be able to cut it, and you won't be here."

I am listening to this man and thinking, "Oh my Lord, what have I gotten myself into?" And I wasn't the only one. When he finished his speech, the reception was over. Everybody went back to the office, because we were too afraid not to. That kind of set the tone for my time at Revlon.

The company's concept of training people was to put you through a constant stream of what I called pop quizzes. Ask the wildest thing you can think of, and if the person doesn't know the answer, criticize him or her for not being prepared. In addition, taking time to explain a project was often seen as unnecessary, because "you should know what to do." I remember the first time my boss did that to me. I had no idea what she asked me to do, because at that stage I did not know the company's unique language, but I will never forget her looking at me as though I was the stupidest person she had ever seen in her life when I asked her to clarify the project.

I swore to myself that this would never happen to me again.

The next time my boss asked me to do something, I took out a pad of paper, wrote down the question, and said, "I'll have the information for you in a couple of hours." I then went to my friend from Avon and had her explain to me what the question meant in terms that I understood. The assignment was simple; I just needed to learn the language.

As I learned and gained confidence, I also gained my boss's trust. We began to work really well together. She would still come up with pop quizzes, but now we could even laugh about them. She would ask me something, and I would say, "Is this pop quiz time or is this something we really need to know?"

The fact of the matter was that the quizzes did prepare me to function within the culture of the company, which was based on the idea of constantly testing you. Charles Revson had instilled in the company the mindset that you excel by rooting out weakness. He would apparently focus on the tiniest details of your business to see how well you knew it. If he found something you didn't know, that became your Achilles' heel, and often the end of your career at the company.

That management style persisted, and everybody was forever trying to figure out what somebody might ask them that they didn't know. This kind of hypervigilance was a constant for me—a familiar part of my impostor fears. For once, though, I didn't feel it was just me. Everyone was in the same boat.

Of course, understanding how tough the environment was didn't prevent me from trying to prove that I could succeed in it. As I had always done when facing difficult situations, I just worked harder. I got to the office by seven or seven-thirty every weekday morning to try and get some things done before the day started, and I never left before nine or ten at night. After two incidents when I left friends stranded at restaurants because meetings were called at the last minute, I stopped even trying to schedule lunch out. I went in to work every Saturday, and spent half the day every Sunday preparing for the week ahead.

The Brass Ring

To me, working on Polished Ambers was a really big deal. But in the context of the rest of the company, it seemed like a pretty small brand that nobody paid much attention to. Or so I thought. A couple of months after I started, Annette called me into her office. She and my boss explained that the person who had been hired to work on the iconic Revlon brand had not worked out and that they wanted me to take it on, temporarily. "People are very impressed with your work, Joyce," she said. "And we want you to handle the brand on an interim basis, until we bring another person on."

I knew this was the biggest gift they could have given me, because it was the biggest brand the company had. "Wow," I thought, "even though I'll have to give it up, I'll really learn a lot here." And I certainly did. Most importantly, I learned how the company worked and how to try to get things done.

I handled the brand for about six months, while the search was underway. The man who was hired to take over permanently came from another beauty company and had a lot of industry experience. He did not, however, understand the Revlon culture. He was under the misconception that as a manager you rely on your people to have all of the details. Well, that wasn't the ethos there. It was your responsibility to know every little detail about even the smallest aspect of your business.

All of this unraveled a little less than a year after he joined the company. We had annual budget meetings where you went before the president of the company and all of his lieutenants. You would sit on one side of this big conference table with your boss, and the president would be in the middle, with his people arrayed around him on the opposite side. Everybody was terrified of these meetings, because, of course, it wasn't just a review of your budget. It was open season, and you were liable to get questions on just about anything. And you had better be prepared. For instance, if you didn't know the market share of your smallest competitor's smallest product, that was treated as a sign that you didn't know your business, and you were raked over the coals.

My presentation was scheduled for two o'clock, and the new director of the Revlon brand was presenting right before me. That afternoon, I was in my office practicing and going through all my data, trying to figure out what they could possibly ask me. A little before two, I got a call, "You're not going to go on yet. They're running late." Five o'clock, same message. Seven o'clock, still the same. At ten o'clock that night, I was finally told that I wasn't going on that day at all. I heard later that the poor man had been grilled until two in the morning. Within two months of that meeting, he was gone.

Again Annette called me into her office, but this time she said, "Would you take the Revlon brand on as a permanent assignment?" I was honored to have my work recognized in this way, and petrified. By this point, I knew just how difficult the company culture made it to accomplish anything. I also knew that I would be held ultimately responsible if I couldn't get the work done, and of course my impostor feelings came rushing in. In spite of these misgivings, I took on the big prize and managed it for a year and a half, until Avon came calling to ask if I would consider coming back.

What's Mine Is Mine

In my two and half years at Revlon, I learned an awful lot about the industry and about myself. I learned how to be a stronger manager and how to take on tough issues and make difficult decisions. But I also began to recognize that my success did not begin and end with me, that I had to rely on other people to accomplish what I needed to get done.

As a marketing director, I had to rely on the support people, the research people, the packaging people. If they didn't back me up, I couldn't get anything done. Fortunately, I had had a great grounding at Avon, which was a really people-oriented company. I treated everyone with respect and forged strong relationships with the key support staff. That helped me, but even so, it was very difficult to move things along. People just didn't work together as teams, because nobody wanted to take responsibility. In a culture so focused on assigning blame, the name of the game becomes passing the buck.

In that environment, even at the height of impostor panics, I had to admit that there were external factors that kept me from living up to what I believed was expected of me. This didn't make the feelings any less intense, but it did guide me in further developing my practice of objectively analyzing the situation to manage the fears.

When I began speaking about the impostor syndrome, I was fascinated to hear about the coping mechanisms other people had developed to help sort through the feelings. Paula Banks Jones, a dear friend whose stellar corporate career included posts as the president of BP Amoco Foundation and as senior vice president for Global Diversity at PepsiCo, spoke very candidly and eloquently about her struggles with impostor fears and shared some profound insights she gained through the years of dealing with them. Paula's description of how she learned to separate her feelings from the facts of the situations she was confronting is particularly powerful in the way it captures the turbulence of the emotions and the need for sober self-examination.

Paula Banks Jones: *A Tape Recorder and a Yellow Legal Pad*

As I was growing up, I always felt a little different, in ways big and small. Right after I was born, for example, my mother found out she couldn't have any more children, so I grew up with my father calling me "Tommy" because he had always wanted a son. Whether to please my father or just because of my own inclination, I gravitated toward things that, back then, girls shied away from: I liked and was good in math, and I had a strong, determined personality.

When I was eight, I was diagnosed with Legg-Perthes, a genetic bone condition, and after surgery spent four years in a wheelchair. During those years, I did not attend a formal school. I went to a handicapped school for a minute, but mostly had home teachers.

My father left my mother just as I returned to school. In those days, having parents that had just gotten divorced was seen as a stigma. So there I was, a chubby teenager just out of a wheelchair going back to school after a very, very long time. But my biggest struggle was being young—I was twelve when I started high school—and out of sync with my peers. I felt so ill at ease that, in spite of my accomplishments, I always thought that failure was just around the corner.

I was in high school when the civil rights movement was picking up momentum, and in Chicago they were beginning to do these educational programs that took African American students to all-white schools to talk about the "Negro experience." Somehow I always found myself on these panels answering questions about what it was like being Black, questions like "Does it wash off?" These conversations started me thinking hard about prejudice and discrimination. I really wanted to know why people have these feelings, and even wrote a paper about it in my junior year. In the process, I went through some very personal turmoil about race.

So when I graduated from college and began working, I was highly sensitized to all the ways in which I felt I didn't fit in. My corporate life began in a management training program at Sears in Oak Brook, a posh suburb of Chicago. There were thirty-three of us in the program. In addition to me, there were two other women and one other African American. The store where we worked had fourteen hundred employees, and the entire staff, counting us trainees, included three Black people.

In that setting, I really struggled with feeling like I didn't belong. The words practically rang in my ears: "I really don't belong, and they're going to find out. They're going to find out."

To prove that I could do this, I worked harder than anybody else. If the work day was eight hours, I'd work twelve. If the standard was that a trainee was supposed to spend six weeks in a smaller store further out in the suburbs, I would spend twelve weeks at two different stores.

The hard work was rewarded. The Oak Brook store, which was the crème de la crème of the Chicago market, only kept on one trainee, and of the thirty-three in my class they kept me and gave me a department to run. That boosted my confidence a little bit, but now I had this tremendous pressure and burden of being "the only one." So often in those situations, you sit at the table and you raise your voice, and it's like nobody hears you.

So I spent a lot of time doubting myself even as I was moving up. At Sears, I went from what would be an hourly job of running a department to a salaried job faster than anyone had ever done it in the history of the company. I was the first and, in many cases, only African American female to do a number of jobs. And still I held on to the conviction that I was advancing because the company needed a token. It couldn't be because I was good. It couldn't be because I was working twelve and fourteen hours a day. It couldn't be because my team respected me and our sales were always beyond what the goals were. I couldn't believe it was any of that, because I still felt that I didn't belong there.

For the next several years, I was promoted every twelve to eighteen months. I always did well and kept getting more opportunities. By the time I was twenty-nine, I had served as the equal opportunity director for the Midwest region of Sears, which included thirteen states, and in the employee relations department for the region, which handled labor relations. That department was staffed by eight white men. When I was hired, they walked into the director's office and threatened to quit if I came on board. To his credit, the man just looked at them and said he would accept their resignations.

However, it was the next assignment that was so challenging it forced me to face up to my feelings of being an impostor. I had been asked to go in as the human resource manager for a facility that was scheduled, unbeknownst to the staff, to be shut down in two years. My job was to keep the employees motivated and productive. It was a tough task, made much, much harder by the person whom I replaced in the human resources job. The man had been promoted into a more senior role, and he sabotaged me, literally, every step of the way and made my life miserable.

Things got so bad, I was feeling beside myself. To keep my sanity, I needed to find a way to release all the stress. I started leaving a tape recorder under the armrest in my car. At the end of the day, when I'd leave work and get off the parking lot, I would stop somewhere quiet, lift up the armrest, take out the tape recorder, and spill out all of my frustration and insecurities onto the tape. Then I would go home and sit at the dining room table with a yellow legal pad divided down the center, with the left side reserved for real issues, and the right for my emotional response. I would turn on the tape recorder and listen to everything I had said that evening, sifting through the things I needed to deal with and the stuff to which I was just overreacting.

This practice allowed me to think through the turmoil of the day. Seeing things in writing helped me get a little objective distance from the situation. And that helped me to say, "I can do this job, and I won't allow myself to become overwhelmed by it." That was the turning point for me.

As Paula's story suggests, to begin to manage through impostor feelings, you first have to gather the courage to look closely at your own fear. When you do, you are likely to find that some of what you are feeling is a perfectly natural reaction to what you are experiencing in your life. You will also see, however, that the feelings of being unfit for your post are, at least in part, a conditioned emotional response to stress. It is really important to learn to make that distinction, because success creates stress by forcing us into unfamiliar territories.

Chapter 8

What If the Naysayers Are Right?

The most debilitating aspect of the impostor syndrome is the way in which it drives us to pursue constantly external validation while fully believing that we don't actually deserve it. To find relief from this terrible burden, it is essential that you learn to use external validation to build your ability to validate yourself.

Developing a realistic sense of your own strengths and limitations is a critical step in confronting your fears about being a fake and the first step in learning to validate yourself. This is much easier to do if you don't go it alone. The next time someone compliments you on something you have done well, see if you can put aside your habitual response and allow the information to sink in. Find trusted allies to help you build self-awareness. Ask them what they think your special gifts are, and listen carefully.

Working on the Revlon brand was an amazing learning experience for me, both professionally and personally. I grew as a marketer and began to develop a more realistic perspective on my own strengths and limitations. I also gained enough confidence to recognize that some environments simply would not be conducive to my success. At Revlon, because the culture made it so difficult to get anything done, I knew that I was not achieving as much as I wanted to, especially considering that I devoted myself entirely to the job. With that, I had made a decision that after three years I would move to another retail beauty company.

Right on schedule, about halfway into my third year at Revlon, I got a call from a marketing executive at Avon. "We're trying to change things up in our marketing area at Avon," he said. "Now that you've got all that experience over there at Revlon, aren't you about ready to come back?"

I said, "No, I don't think I want to come back. I like the company but I really enjoy doing consumer marketing, and that is not Avon's focus."

The next thing I knew, I got a call from Jack Lausten, the man who had done so much to help advance my career at Avon. "Let's have lunch," he said, and I agreed, praying that there were no last-minute meetings on the day I was scheduled to see him.

Over lunch, Jack said, "Look, a lot has changed since you left. I know that you want to do consumer marketing. Well, that's what we're trying to do."

Jack explained that a real shift had taken place in the way Avon saw its business. Before I left, we were essentially marketing to the sales organization not to the consumer. As more and more women were going into the workforce, the company recognized that its consumer base was undergoing a profound change. Women weren't at home anymore, and they were buying products wherever they happened to be. It was now imperative to reach the consumer directly.

"That's where we're taking the marketing organization," Jack continued. "And we think that you can make a big difference."

Of course, it was a real boost to my ego to be courted for my skills. Jack paused to gauge my reaction and then added, "This will also position you well to become a vice president of the company."

Even by this point, there had only been a couple of women officers at Avon, and only one African American male who had risen to that level. No Black woman had ever held such a post; and there had never been an African American vice president of marketing, male or female. Simply to be on the high-potential list for such a job was huge.

"Well, I am honored," I told Jack, "and it will be great working for you again."

In a couple of days, I went into my boss's office and gave her my resignation, with two weeks' notice. She seemed so flustered, she didn't know what to say. Soon after I got to my desk, though, Annette, our group vice president, came by and said, "Oh, Joyce, I can't believe you're actually going to leave." After that, no one said another word, and I continued to get ready to go.

A couple of days before my last day, the president of the division asked to meet with me and said, "I can't believe you're actually going to do this. We've got big things in mind for you here."

"You know, John," I told him, thinking it was pretty late in the game to begin talking about a counteroffer, "I really appreciate what you're telling me, but it's too hard to get anything done here. I work these incredible hours, and I never really feel like I get much accomplished. I feel like I can do more at Avon."

I could hardly believe this was Joyce speaking. I knew I had gotten tougher at Revlon, but I hadn't quite realized that a part of that was a new directness. I still tried to be respectful and diplomatic, but now I spoke my mind.

I'm Not What You Expected

Once at Avon, I quickly saw that my new interpersonal skills would stand me in good stead. I returned as a director, heading up the gift business and reporting to Jack Lausten, who was then the vice president of marketing for the gift business. As luck would have it, he was transferred within months of my being back, and the other Jack, who had made my life so uncomfortable on the Canadian business, took over as our vice president.

"I can't believe you brought me back to report to this person," I said to Jack when he told me the news.

"Well, I'm going to tell him that you don't really want to work for him," he replied.

And I said, "Thanks, but I think I can handle it."

I went in and had a heart-to-heart with my new/old boss. "Look," I said, "you need to know that I am a very different person from when I left." I wanted him to know that I now had a level of confidence; that I wasn't just going to take what he said and then find somebody to help me.

"If you have problems with something I'm doing," I told

him, "I'm strong enough for you to tell me that. And if I have problems with what you're doing, I will let you know as well."

We ended up working well together, and I never forgot how powerful a tool direct, clear communication is in building relationships with people.

Avon was, indeed, changing, both in its focus and its structure. There was a lot of movement within the company, and I was clearly on an upward trajectory. Within a year of coming back, I was promoted to senior director, overseeing the gift and decorative business. The next step would be vice president, when the right position opened up.

A major opportunity presented itself when the senior vice president of marketing, who had come from Europe, returned home. Avon always promoted from within, but this time the executive team decided to bring in a senior marketing officer from outside the company. They also announced that, as part of the reconfiguration of marketing, our vice president was also going to be transferred elsewhere. This was huge. It was the chance I had worked so hard for. And I thought that I had a good shot at getting the job, given what I had been told when Avon was wooing me to come back.

No sooner than the announcement was made, though, it became clear that things were much more complicated. My counterpart on the beauty business, Jim, who was a good friend and someone I had hired out of business school when I was manager of merchandising, had been selected to provide support to the new senior vice president during the transition period, to help him while he learned the company. It seemed clear that Jim was being positioned for promotion into our boss's spot. He was the heir apparent.

I stayed true to my word and went to talk to our vice president. "Is this a message, Jack?" I asked him. "Does this signal that Jim is going to be the next vice president?"

Although we had by now figured out how to work together, Jack did not like direct confrontations. He simply refused to answer me and told me that I needed to go and talk to the departing senior vice president.

I got along really well with our senior vice president, Alan, so I went to him and asked the same question. "Well, that's one of the scenarios," he said. He wouldn't come out and say it point blank, but it was clear that was the direction in which things were moving.

I was mulling this over when Alan surprised me by asking, "How would you compare yourself to Jim and Mike?" (Mike was another colleague who was a director in the merchandising area.)

This was not the moment to be self-effacing. "I brought Jim into the company," I said, "and I trained him. I think I know both merchandising and marketing better than he does. Mike is probably a stronger merchant, but I believe I'm a much stronger product marketing person because of my internal and external experience."

Alan nodded his agreement and said, "Well, I can't necessarily argue with that, but you know, Joyce, they're just more comfortable with Jim."

"Oh God," I thought, "give me a break." I worked hard. I did everything I could to make the business successful. I delivered results. To have all that dismissed and to have the decision about promotion pivot on how comfortable the senior executives felt with me was just not fair.

My impostor fears focused on the ways in which I might be underprepared because of my race, gender, and economic background. Suddenly, I had to contend with the fact that I may be denied opportunities simply because I didn't look like the people in charge.

"Look, Alan," I said, this time not even trying to hide my anger. "I'm Black, and I'm a woman, those things I can't change. I've done everything I can to make people feel comfortable with me."

"Well, don't do anything rash," he said.

"No, I'm not going to do anything rash," I replied. "I like Jim, and we've always been great colleagues. I will tell you though, if that's what happens, I'm not going to resign that day, but I will be looking."

The Agony of Victory

The company made a Solomonic decision. They created a new structure and promoted both Jim and me to vice president. He was in charge of marketing for the beauty business, and I headed up marketing and purchasing for the gifts and the jewelry business.

Jim Preston, who was the president of the U.S. organization, called me into his office to tell me about the promotion personally. "Joyce, I know you," he said. "You're going to worry about what happens to other women and African Americans coming up behind you if you mess up. My advice is, just don't take that on."

I was a little taken aback that Jim saw so clearly into what was in my heart. But it was good advice. I was, of course, elated.

At the same time, though, I was scared to death. I had put myself out there, had said that I wanted this role and that I deserved it. Now, I was filled with doubt about my ability to cut it. All the hard work that had come before didn't seem to count for much, and I was consumed with worries about whether I was good enough to manage this job.

The fact that I was the first African American woman to make officer at Avon added an element of public interest to the situation that exponentially increased the level of pressure I felt. Inside the company, the Black Employees Network, which had now become a stand-alone employee group, gave a huge party in my honor and presented me with a beautiful painting for my new office. The amount of pride people expressed was so touching. I just wish I had been able to enjoy it for what it was, without also feeling dragged down by the weight of expectation that it seemed to carry.

The extensive press coverage just added to my fear of now being in the public eye. This was 1985, and the promotion of an African American woman to the level of officer in a Fortune 500 company was big news. (Unfortunately, things haven't changed nearly as much as we all had hoped back then.) Even my hometown paper, *The Times-Picayune,* ran a "local-woman-makes-good" story. It was wonderful to get all the congratulations from friends and family, and it made me that much more concerned about falling on my face.

All I could hear in my mind was, "Oh my goodness, if I fail at this, it is going to be a huge failure."

I could picture the failure very clearly. My business does not perform, and I am fired from the company. And then what do I do? When I had gone to Columbia, I had had a fallback plan. I could go home and teach school. At this stage, the failure would be complete, and public. I would be exposed as an impostor. What would the headlines be then? Would another African American get the same chance in the future? It was awful to think about giving ammunition to people who insisted that people who looked like me were inherently unsuited for leadership.

At the very heart of this fear was the knowledge that I couldn't work any harder than I already was doing. I had always responded to new challenges by working more, putting in extra hours, doing additional prep. In this new position, I was going to be managing many more people, overseeing units I knew nothing about, and functioning in a peer group that had never included anyone like me. And I was terrified that I didn't have enough of the smarts to succeed in this bigger role.

One of the major dangers the impostor syndrome poses for those of us who experience it is the isolation it imposes on us. I felt that if I admitted that there were things I didn't know, people would question whether I deserved the job. And now the fear was magnified, because if I showed weakness, "they" might say, "We knew we shouldn't have given her that chance. We knew that somebody Black could not really do this." So I worked twice as hard to project an aura of confidence, all the while questioning my ability to handle the pressure.

Day of Reckoning

A major test of my ability to handle the job and its pressures came about six months after I had been promoted. We were working on a big new gift product for children for the Christmas season. At Avon, we did most of the product development and production ourselves, but occasionally a vendor would bring a good idea, and we would source the product from them. This was one such situation, where a vendor had developed a new technology to produce sponges that were impregnated with soap. We liked the idea and designed Muppet sponges—Kermit and Miss Piggy.

The vendor was handling production. So rather than being able to manage quality control, we had to rely on product samples. We got product in at different stages of production and tested it. Everything was working fine, and we were getting ready to launch the product in about two months.

We took the product into a test phase before going national in order to estimate the sales volume. The Muppet sponges, according to our research, were poised to be a huge hit, with sales of over a million units in the first two weeks.

Just before launch, the vendor informed us that they were in a legal dispute with the subcontractor who was producing the sponges. They assured us that they had already begun working with another company and that there would not be any problems getting the product to market on time. What they didn't tell us right away was that the original subcontractor had refused to turn over the production formula, which meant that the new factory was starting from scratch. We found that out when the next batch of samples arrived and, much to our dismay, the heads started popping off the sponge characters when you squeezed them.

This was a horror scenario. We were two weeks out from national launch. I had a million of these things on order. And I was going to have Miss Piggy's and Kermit's heads popping off in the bathtub with the kids. I was panicking. If we missed the shipping dates on this, I felt that my career would basically implode.

We were now getting samples from every single production run. By the weekend before launch, the heads were still popping off. Friday morning, I went into my boss' office and told him that I was taking a team from research & development and production into the vendor's plant that afternoon and that we would work the entire weekend to attempt to solve the issue. If we couldn't fix it, we would have to take the product off sale.

We flew in on a small propeller-driven plane and went directly from the airport into the plant. We didn't leave the plant until midday on Saturday, when we finally went to the hotel to check in and take a shower. Then we went back to work. We didn't sleep for two days, but by the afternoon on Sunday, we had a formula that was working. Now the issue was that the workers in the plant didn't have the expertise to produce the volume of product we needed. I called in people from an Avon production site to take over the lines. By Sunday night, when we went back to New York, we were producing in large enough quantities to allow the product to go on sale.

Throughout the entire episode, my boss was very supportive. And he was very complimentary about the way I had handled the problem. Even I had to admit that I had done well in a difficult situation. I had never handled production before, and in retrospect, at first I had been too hands-off with the vendor. But once I realized there was a problem, I knew what needed to be done and was able to get the right people in place to do the job. That experience of facing a major potential failure early in my time as a senior executive helped me to begin to recognize my own strengths. And with that, the conversation with my impostor fears began to change too.

Learning to Know Yourself

As we succeed and advance in our careers, we inevitably encounter situations that challenge our abilities. We also cross paths with honest critics, powerful competitors, and out-and-out enemies. Running into roadblocks can cause feelings of doubt and unworthiness but it also provides opportunities for true growth.

The real difficulty with the impostor syndrome is that it is very much like a kind of metabolic disorder. It makes us hungry for external validation, but makes it impossible for us to draw sustenance from it. We simply can never have enough to quiet our fears. That only becomes possible when we begin to accept our actual strengths and weaknesses and to learn how to derive internal validation from that self-knowledge.

I got to know Val Ackerman, the founding president of the WNBA and former president of USA Basketball, when she joined the Girls Inc. board of directors. From our first meeting, I was taken with her quiet intensity and incredible skills as a listener. I was also really touched by her dedication to helping young people succeed.

When I began to write and speak about my experience with the impostor syndrome, Val told me that she has also struggled with these feelings, particularly with respect to her intellectual abilities. She also spoke very movingly about her own journey of conquering the feelings through the process of self-discovery.

Val Ackerman: *If I Can't Be the Smartest, I'll Be the Hardest-Working*

I grew up in New Jersey, in a suburb of Trenton, the elder of two kids. My parents were solidly middle-class. My mom worked in state government in New Jersey, and my dad was a high school athletic director, and later a gym teacher and a referee at the high school level. He was all sports, and he was really my inspiration. He was very encouraging and took my athletic interest as seriously as he took my brother's. Both my parents were great about always supporting us in pursuing what we wanted to do.

I became interested in sports at a very young age. This was the mid- and late 1960s, so there weren't many opportunities for girls— no leagues to join or travel teams to be part of. You just played in the backyard. My dad was the guy throwing footballs and baseballs with me. He put up a basketball hoop in the driveway, where I shot a million baskets. I was in high school when I got my first chance to play on a team. I was so excited, I played field hockey, basketball, and ran track.

After high school, I focused on basketball. I went to the University of Virginia on an athletic scholarship and played ball on the varsity team. After college, I played professionally in France. It was wonderful, because I got to play basketball and to see the world at the same time.

Even though I loved sports, my lifelong dream, from an early age, was to become a lawyer. I am not really sure why. It just sounded interesting and lofty. So after a year in Europe, I came back to the United States and went to law school at UCLA.

I was very eager to get a job in sports coming out of law school, but they were hard to come by. I went to work at a big Wall Street law firm back in New York, and then, after two years, was fortunate to land a job in the legal department at the National Basketball Association. That was a dream come true for me to have that professional opportunity. Everything just came together, my passion for basketball and my professional aspirations.

But I had a really hard time with my feelings of intellectual intimidation. This was kind of a theme for me. At every stage of my life, I was surrounded by really smart people. In college, there were a lot of bright students. In law school, you are dealing with really brainy classmates. At my law firm, there were many brilliant people. And at the NBA, we had some of the sharpest people in sports, led by David Stern, who is supremely intelligent.

My way of coping with these feelings was to work harder than anyone else. I said to myself that since I wasn't the smartest person in the room, I would be the most diligent one. On every assignment I put in extra time, did as much research as possible, and made sure I understood all the details. Before every meeting, I prepared for hours.

The preparation paid off, and I did well in the intellectually challenging climate of the NBA. I started out as a staff lawyer and then moved over to the commissioner's office after about eighteen months. I worked on a variety of projects, but my role was not very clearly defined. This wasn't really an issue until I had my two children. At that point, I went through a very difficult time professionally.

There weren't many women working at the NBA at that point who had had children and stayed. The senior management were all men, and for the most part they had wives who didn't work. That was the norm. My husband is a lawyer, so people suspected money wasn't going to be an issue for me, and they didn't expect me to come back after my pregnancies. I felt I had to prove to them that even though I was a mother of infants, I was really serious about my career. There was some real tension that I had to fight through.

I was already used to being one of the hardest-working people in the room, so I wasn't afraid of the challenge. With time, my colleagues came to see just how committed I was to my career and to basketball.

My major break came when the commissioner wanted to look at women's basketball in a serious way. He asked me to lead that effort, which resulted in our supporting the women's Olympic basketball team at the Atlanta games. That was the testing ground to get a sense of the level of interest in a women's league. We got a lot of encouragement from fans and sponsors, and eventually launched the WNBA in the summer of 1997. I was truly honored to be selected and to serve as president of the league for the first eight years.

When I became the president of the WNBA, I didn't have the same kinds of doubts I had experienced earlier in my career. It felt like a cause, and I saw the real sense of purpose and a clearly defined leadership role for myself. It was very empowering and certainly a confidence boost.

And, of course, it was exciting and intimidating, all at once, because it was new. Now, though, I really did feel like I knew what I was doing. I certainly had the basketball background, and, from having been at the league for as long as I had, I understood how our company worked. I also began to acknowledge my personal strengths, beyond just being a hard worker. For example, I try to be a good listener. I recognized that I have a humility that helps me make good decisions, because I don't think I am always right and therefore take other people's opinions into account. And most importantly, I gave myself credit for being good with people, for knowing how to build a team and make people feel empowered. Years after I left, I would bump into people who had worked with me who'd say, "It was so important to me that you included me in all those meetings. I can't tell you how much better I was able to do my job."

I think it was when I began to appreciate these qualities in myself that I understood just how much I had grown. Building the self-awareness to figure out how you can maximize what you can contribute based on your strengths is a critical part of professional development. Whenever I give speeches now, I always say to young people, "There are always going to be people out there who are smarter than you, and people who are going to work harder than you. You may not be able to make yourself smarter. And, beyond a certain point, you may not be able to work any harder. But if you look at yourself, you can figure out what your special strengths are. You may be a great public speaker. You may have personal charm. Or you might have a wonderful sense of humor. Whatever your strengths are, find them, and put them to good use."

Whatever coping mechanisms we develop to help us deal with our impostor fears, sooner or later we reach their limitations. For me that moment of truth came when I realized, after stepping into my new vice president role at Avon, that I simply could not work any harder. At that point, I had to evaluate honestly my ability to do the job. That was the beginning for me of learning how to manage the impostor syndrome from a position of strength.

Chapter 9

The Weight of the World

In large part, the impostor syndrome is fed by the mistaken belief many of us hold that our value is measured by some "objective" yardstick. We do not recognize our essential worth and are therefore constantly terrified that we will be found lacking. The pursuit of validation becomes a driving need, often eclipsing other parts of our lives and ourselves.

The process of conquering these fears begins with stopping to look at your life and asking what might be missing for you. Ask whether you are satisfied. Are there dimensions you want to add? Do you need more balance? Ultimately, the question has to be, "What do I value about myself?"

The public attention I began to receive when I became an officer at Avon was a mixed blessing. I found that I really enjoyed speaking to groups of people—especially younger people. I was happy to share my insights with people or simply show them that there were opportunities in the world for people who looked like me.

Media stories, on the other hand, often felt like that much

extra pressure. It was nice to get the external recognition, but it really didn't feel like much of a validation. Journalists were writing about me because I was a "first," not because I was great at my job. So the stories didn't make me feel more assured, they just made me that much more afraid of failing.

The attention from the press, however, did lead to a surprising insight and to a major change in my life. Shortly after I had been named vice president at Avon, a woman reporter was interviewing me for an executive profile. As we finished talking about my background and career, she asked, in a very matter-of-fact way, "Well, when did you decide not to get married and have children?"

That really brought me up short. It certainly hadn't been an intentional decision. I was so focused on my work, I had simply never thought about it. And now I felt like I had to step back and really look at my life.

In New York, as I guess is the case in all big cities, people tend to function in groups, as compared to smaller places, where social life is much more about couples getting together. I had a circle of really good friends, people who knew and loved me for who I am. Most of them, both men and women, were not married, and we all hung out together. The fact that I was not in a relationship or even seeing anybody on a steady basis had never entered my psyche. Even when I had events where I needed a date, I always had a friend who would go with me.

After that conversation with the reporter, I had to admit that I was basically consumed with the job. That was, to a large degree, the norm for women in business. By the mid-1980s, there were many articles in the media highlighting how few women who had gone into the corporate world were married or had children. People now talk a lot about work–life balance. As I thought about what I wanted for my life, it wasn't so much balance but an added dimension.

Once I admitted that to myself, I had to start thinking about how I would go about meeting someone. I spent most of my time at work, and there was no one there I was interested in. (Besides, I wasn't at all sure how I would have felt about dating somebody at the company.) So I realized that if, in fact, I did want to have a relationship, I had to do more than just become open to the idea, I was going to have to put some effort into it.

Well, as I have learned, you put an intention out into the universe, and things begin to happen. Around a year or so after I started thinking about all this, Johnie came back to New York. We had stayed in touch over the years after business school, through occasional phone calls to catch up. I had always enjoyed his company—particularly his sly sense of humor—and it was good to have him among our group of friends again.

Johnie had come to New York with the idea of finishing his classwork and dissertation to complete the requirements for the dual-degree (MBA/Ed.D) program that he had been enrolled in at Columbia. I learned that he and his wife were separated, but I was cautious about getting involved. After about a year, however, he got a divorce, and we began seeing each other, which led to a committed relationship.

By this point, Johnie had made the decision to leave higher education. He moved to Dayton, Ohio, and took over human resources and labor relations at an automotive sequencing company owned by his aunt and uncle. So we just commuted between Ohio and New York. Although, I have to be honest, mostly he came to New York.

Never Look Back

Work continued to be the central concern in my life, even though I was now in a serious relationship. I was consumed with not only excelling at the job I had but also with making sure I had the opportunity to advance. I wasn't interested in just bigger titles, I wanted to work in areas I hadn't tried before and take on larger responsibilities. So I wasn't at all happy when, shortly after the Muppet sponge episode, our senior vice president asked me to move over to the struggling merchandising department to fix the problems they were having. I had been in merchandising from the time I joined Avon until I left for Revlon, and I wasn't excited about going back to it. It didn't really sink in at the time that the request was a vote of confidence, a signal that I was seen as someone who got things done.

I agreed to take on the post of vice president of merchandising on the condition that I would return to the product side after the department was back on track. That took about two years. A bright spot in my move back to merchandising was that I now also had responsibility for the creative department that produced the Avon brochure. That was exciting, since I had never handled that area. But the real prize came up a short while later, when the top marketing position on the beauty business became available.

At that point, Avon was about a four-billion-dollar company. Sixty percent of the revenue came from beauty products, and the gift and jewelry businesses each accounted for twenty percent. Beauty, in other words, was the core business, and that's where I wanted to be. I wanted to be considered for the job and was deeply disappointed when the senior executive team decided to conduct a search for someone from outside the company. As it happened, after a year of searching failed to turn up the kind of person the top brass thought they wanted, they offered the position to me, and I became vice president of marketing for cosmetics, fragrances, and toiletries. And not too long after that, I became vice president of all product marketing.

Even though I was doing well in a position I enjoyed, as usual I was already beginning to think about what would be next. I am not sure I fully articulated it even to myself, but I felt as if I had to prepare to move out of marketing and into a general management role. I was aware that a couple of people at the company had attended the senior executive program at Harvard, and I decided that I also wanted to do one of these programs to gain broader skills.

Rick Goings had taken over as the president of the U.S. business the year before, and he and I had really hit it off. When I told him that I wanted to get some additional training, he gave me the go-ahead. I researched the options offered by the top business schools and chose the Stanford Executive Program. It was an intensive, six-week summer course, and I loved it. I felt intellectually challenged, engaged, and completely at ease. Even though I had had the familiar misgivings about my abilities and the fear of competing with senior executives from around the world, once I was on campus and started working, I knew I was exactly where I wanted to be.

At Stanford they told us that many people do not go back to the same job as the one they left. Well, I was planning to go back to my job. To my surprise, though, the job had changed, the marketing area had gone through another restructuring, and I was now reporting to a new senior vice president of marketing, who until then had been my counterpart in merchandising. I felt as if I had taken a step backward, instead of preparing to move forward, and was not very happy.

Things got back on track about a year and a half later when my boss transferred to Europe, and I became the senior vice president of marketing. From there, it got even more interesting as we went through a work redesign process to put in a global structure. For the first time in Avon's history, select brands were defined as global brands and as such would be managed by a new global marketing group. These were all major brands, with minimum worldwide sales of upward of $50 million. In the past, individual countries had a lot of latitude about how to handle products. Now, the global brands were under the control of the new organization we had created.

I was thrilled to be named vice president of global marketing. With the exception of my brief experience in Canada, I had never worked on Avon's international business before. Even more importantly, I was really excited about the breadth of responsibility I had in that role. In the new structure, along with my counterpart in Europe, I was in charge of these huge global brands and oversaw the marketing strategy around the world.

From the start, though, it was clear that there were problems with this way of doing business. The United States and Europe, which were the two major Avon markets then, were none too pleased about having to take orders from somebody in global. They felt that they were so big that they should have control of all brands in their market and didn't want to be told how to do things or to have things done for them. So Jim Preston, who was now the CEO, frequently had to mediate one big issue or another. Finally, after about a year and a half, Jim said, "This is not working. We need to rethink this structure."

When I realized that the global marketing job was going to lose line responsibility and focus exclusively on strategy, I decided that what I really wanted to do was to take on a general management role in one of the countries where Avon had operations. I went to the head of human resources, Marcia Worthing, who was a friend, and asked her confidentially whether she saw any country positions opening up in the near future. She explained that there had been a lot of staff changes when the global structure was put in place and that there wasn't likely to be anything suitable for me any time soon.

Suddenly, I had to consider the possibility that I would have to leave Avon if I wanted to continue to grow and progress. That was disappointing and scary. I hadn't looked for a job since I had graduated from business school. If I had looked at any opportunities, they were ones suggested by executive recruiters, and lately even those had been mostly for corporate boards.

"Joyce," I said to myself, "what do you do now?"

Through a friend, I was introduced to John Lucht, a consultant who advised senior executives on career transitions. I met with him and even went to get tested at one of those companies that helps you figure out what you are really good at. I had just read *The Celestine Prophecy*, and it was kind of exciting to think about discovering some latent talent that I might have suppressed. The tests basically told me that I was good at what I did, but by this point the idea of striking out and exploring new directions had become really compelling.

I had not yet found my next challenge, but I knew that it was time to leave Avon. I let the company know and worked with them to make the transition as smooth as possible. At the end of 1994, I resigned from the company, ending my eighteen-year career there.

More to Prove

A lot of people thought that I had lost my mind when I left Avon without having another job. Most of them didn't know that I had been preparing for a year. I had worked with John on a strategy, had crafted a five-page resume that documented with statistics my achievements over the years, and had a comprehensive list of top-notch executive recruiters who worked in the industries I was interested in.

I had decided that I definitely wanted a general management position and that I was ready to try something other than beauty. I was particularly interested in telecommunications. This was a time when the newly created regional phone companies were just starting to do consumer marketing, and I felt that it would an interesting place to be. But I was open to other industries, and flexible about location.

I took a week or two off after I wrapped up my job and then went to work, nearly full-time, sending out resumes and talking to search firms. I had a pretty high profile and a good reputation, so opportunities started to present themselves quickly. The one I was particularly excited about was with Bell Atlantic, as president of the consumer division. After several rounds of interviews, I was one of the finalists. Ultimately, though, the company chose an internal candidate.

Of course, you never know how things work out. Shortly after my disappointing experience with Bell Atlantic, I got a call from a search firm representing Ray Chambers, the prominent private-equity investor who had made his name with the buyout of Avis in 1985, among other notable deals. A native of Newark, Ray wanted to develop a network of direct-selling companies to create financial opportunities for people in poor neighborhoods, and he wanted my help. After a few meetings, I knew that this was not quite the right fit. I told Ray that I liked the concept and that I would work with him to refine the strategy but that I would not join the project for the long term.

Well, as they say, when one door closes another one opens. Ray was an investor in Morningside Capital, an investment group led by his former associate Vince Wasik, which was in the final stages of purchasing Carson Products, the leading manufacturer of African American hair care products. Morningside was putting together a management team to run the company after the buyout, and Ray suggested that they speak with me.

Carson was a privately owned business in Savannah, Georgia. It had been in the hands of the Minis family for over forty years, ever since the patriarch, Abram Minis, bought a tiny manufacturing company, renamed it, and built it into a thriving corporation by focusing on the needs of Black consumers. Mr. Minis was now in his nineties, and the rest of the family had decided that it was time to sell the business. Dr. Leroy (Roy) Keith, former president of Morehouse College, who sat on Carson's board, saw an opportunity to grow an already preeminent company serving the African American market. He brought in Morningside Capital, and they were well on their way to closing the deal.

After I met with Vince and did my research on Carson, I became more and more excited about the opportunity. The company had the number one brand in ethnic hair care, they had the leading brand of ethnic shave, and their growth was impressive. The strategy Morningside had developed was also really interesting. They were planning on aggressively expanding in Africa, Europe, the Caribbean, and South America; entering the professional salon sector; and launching a cosmetics line to build on the strength of the *Dark and Lovely* brand.

In our conversations, the folks from Morningside explained that they wanted a new management team with the skills to implement their strategy. They wanted me to come in as the executive vice president of marketing, a position they saw as critical to the international expansion and to the leveraging of the company's brands. I told them that I was interested in joining the team, but only as the president. Ultimately, we struck a compromise, agreeing that I would become president after the man who had been there for many years retired in a year's time.

With the good advice of John Lucht, I negotiated a five-year contract that stipulated that I was in line to become president after one year. If that didn't come to pass, I would be at liberty to break the contract and would be entitled to a financial settlement. I also negotiated for a small equity interest in the company. With that, I signed on and got to work.

All of this happened really quickly. We had started the conversations in March of 1995, and the deal was supposed to close in May. So, as soon as I started, I had to immerse myself in the details. I went down to Savannah as part of the team doing final due diligence. While there, I also started looking around for a place to live.

Most deals rarely close right on schedule. The Carson deal

was finally signed in August, and we really had to move fast to keep things running. The closing was on a Thursday, and I had to be in place in Savannah by the following Monday. I packed a couple of bags and flew down. I had found a house in Savannah, but it wouldn't be finished until October, so in the meantime I made do in long-term lodgings for business travelers.

It really didn't matter where I lived, because, almost immediately, we started traveling widely, both in the United States and internationally. Within two months, we were in South Africa buying a manufacturing plant, because the business was growing so fast. I didn't have time to move into my new house until December.

The pace at which we were working was, at times, unnerving, but exhilarating. When we went to South Africa, we met with banks to finance the plant purchase. During the discussions, the banks got very interested in our ethnic hair care business. In light of the growth we were experiencing in South Africa, Nigeria, and Ghana, they urged us to consider going public on the Johannesburg Stock Exchange. There had never been a business that focused on Black South Africans listed on the exchange, and the finance people estimated that an initial public offering would be very successful.

So, less than six months after the closing, we were in the midst of creating a prospectus. By the early spring, we were in South Africa and Europe doing a road show for the initial public offering. I had never done anything like that before, and it was an exciting challenge talking to people about investing in the business while at the same time trying to grow the business. Less than a year after we had stepped in, the company was public in South Africa.

Taking on the World

So here I was, now president and COO of a rapidly growing international company. I had gotten exactly what I wanted, a chance to manage a business. Nevertheless, the familiar fear of not being up to the job still lingered. Roy, who was the chairman and CEO, and I made a good team. He had limited experience running a business but was very good at managing the investors and our external relationships, and he valued my experience and gave me wide latitude to run the day-to-day operations. That, however, intensified the pressure in its own way.

As we have observed, that's the conundrum of the impostor syndrome. It drives us to take on more and more responsibility to prove we are capable. And yet, as we reach higher and achieve more, the weight of the fear also grows.

Ron Parker, PepsiCo's retired chief global diversity and inclusion officer and senior vice president of human resources and labor relations, speaks especially eloquently about the personal price we pay in pursuing this drive for success on ever-larger fields of endeavor. I met Ron through our mutual friend Dr. Ella Bell, and he was very generous in sharing his experiences and insights. I was particularly touched by his account of taking decisive action to mitigate the effects of the impostor syndrome on his life.

Ron Parker: *Returning to Myself*

I grew up, the middle of five children, on a family ranch in Brenham, Texas, a small German town about seventy-five miles west of Houston. Through eighth grade, our schools were segregated. But then in 1968, the school systems integrated. That first year of high school, many of us walked in with a bit of a chip on our shoulders. It was clear this wasn't our school. And while the school tried to make us feel included, we initially felt like tenants.

Sports were a big thing in the community. We broke down a lot of racial barriers by performing well on the field of play, creating an atmosphere of inclusion. I played football and got a lot of affirmation through that. During my senior year, I was the class president and was voted the most likely to succeed in college and in life. I went to Blinn College on a scholarship and then to Texas Christian University and played tight end for both.

Out of TCU, I was drafted by the Chicago Bears. My NFL career was cut short, though. I played up until the first game, and then injured my knee. I came back to the Fort Worth area and was headed to Southern Methodist University Law School. My plan was to become a lawyer and to use my athletic platform to make some change in the world.

At this point, I was a little full of myself: star athlete, good pupil, local community leader, young, tall, good-looking. I had it all, but in many ways I was uncertain about who I was. And that got me a bit sidetracked when an opportunity presented itself for me to enter the world of business.

That's when I first had my first encounter of what it's like to feel like an impostor. I accepted a position as the head of relocation services for an oil services company. I was moving people around the country, selling their homes, buying new homes. I was responsible for hundreds of thousands of dollars, and I had no real estate background, nothing that qualified me as a professional in this area. For the first time in my life, I felt like I didn't know what I was doing, and I was sure I would get discovered at any moment.

To compensate, I studied my tail off. I would come home and immerse myself in real estate literature. I signed up for as many professional real estate classes as I could. All the while, I was actually doing the work. I had assembled a good team, and we were getting the job done. And that allowed me to fake confidence.

I eventually moved into the human resources area and then was recruited by PepsiCo. And again I got myself into a situation where I felt I was in over my head. You have to remember, I am wired as an athlete. Sometimes we, as athletes, have a tendency to push the boundaries, and it can get us in trouble from time to time by doing things that are very risk oriented. Going into PepsiCo, I told them I wanted to be in labor relations, for which I had very little formal training. The culture at PepsiCo is very entrepreneurial, and I suddenly found myself, with limited expertise, out there on my own, the human resources manager of a plant of eight hundred to a thousand people.

Again I felt like I had no business being where I was. I was at the table with a group of peers who were leading sales, marketing, finance, legal, operations, and engineering. They all had degrees in their given areas, and I was a tall, good-looking, very personable, ex-football player with no formal credentials or job experience behind me in my area of labor relations. Each day, month, and quarter, I was sure I was going to be exposed.

But as an athlete you are also taught to push yourself. I drew upon those natural instincts to step up my game. And I surrounded myself with very, very, very talented people.

After I had been with the company two years, PepsiCo asked me to move to the corporate headquarters in New York as manager of staffing. All of the senior vice presidents and vice presidents were there, and this young man from Brenham, Texas, was now dealing on a daily basis with folks who had MBAs and Ph.Ds from Columbia, Yale, and the University of Pennsylvania.

Suddenly, I felt that I was among people who perceived athletes as being dumb, inexperienced, one-dimensional, you name it. I found myself not mentioning that I had played sports. If someone asked me directly, I would ignore the question, because I did not want to be labeled. I had enough to deal with just feeling inadequate in this highly intellectual, entrepreneurial culture. I did not want to add to that by saying, "Oh yes, I was a star football player back in college and high school."

This was a whole new world for me. I liked what I saw there, and I wanted to stay. I was very concerned about anything that could get me uninvited. That feeling was particularly acute, since I was one of a very few African Americans at the corporate office at that time.

And I started to change. I started to become more like the people whose judgments I feared rather than myself. I started to dress like them, walk like them, talk like them, so I'd blend in.

I lost myself in the company. I was so bent on not being exposed that I spent a lot of time at the office, working extra hours, working really hard, being away from my family. My wife would ask, "Why are you working so late all the time?" And I just felt that I could not run the risk of not being prepared.

So I worked, and I earned a reputation throughout PepsiCo as being one of the hardest-working executives to ever come through the company. But I paid dearly for it. To this day, my relationship with our middle child, our son, suffers from the fact that for the first years of his life I was so immersed in trying to be someone I wasn't that I did not spend time with him. I lost contact with some of my friends, and I became very angry with myself because I didn't like what I was becoming.

I was group director at the time, and my next role would have been vice president. And I tell you, I was nervous. I was nervous about moving to that next level. The higher you ascend, the greater the fear you have of being discovered, and the greater the potential downfall.

I chose to leave PepsiCo in 1984, because I needed to rediscover myself. I was out of the organization for a year, and during that time I found validation in my ability to be a learner. I also realized that a lot of my colleagues were lacking in certain areas where I was very strong. To some degree, I was no different from them, and they were no different from me. We all have some strengths and some weaknesses. "Does that make me a fraud?" I had to ask. "Does that make me any less valuable to an enterprise or to myself?" And the answer, of course, was, "no."

With that renewed sense of myself, I was proud to accept the invitation to return to PepsiCo. I made vice president within the year, and from there I just kept moving up in the company, finally to the role of senior vice president. But I never let myself forget to be just me.

For those of us who experience impostor fears, the need to keep moving and accomplishing can feel like a compulsion. There is always more to prove, or, as a friend put it, "another dragon to slay."

The further we travel in meeting this need, however, the greater the sacrifices we have to make. And often, we find that things that are important to us are missing from our lives. At times, as Ron describes, we do not even recognize or like who we are.

Chapter 10

What Did You Do to Get Here?

It isn't easy to stop worrying about what other people think of you. It is particularly difficult if you don't think very much of yourself. The impostor syndrome can feel like a kind of amnesia, one that makes us forget our own accomplishments. The only way to counter it is to consistently ask yourself the question: What did I do to get here? And here is the tricky part, you not only have to ask the question but also answer it honestly and without false modesty.

Practice seeing other people as they are. See their strengths and weaknesses. That will allow you to see yourself in the same way, with compassion and understanding.

In the higher echelons of the business world, many people aspire to positions on corporate boards. Toward the end of my tenure at Avon, as I began thinking about moving into general management, I also contemplated the possibility of joining a board. In fact, I received inquiries from search firms about a couple of potential positions. The one I was most interested in was Timberland, but unfortunately, after a series of conversations, the company decided not to bring on another outside director.

The next opportunity came up shortly after I became president of Carson. SNET (Southern New England Telephone Company) was looking for someone with marketing expertise and the search firm they hired approached me. After the vetting process, they invited me to join the board. And, boy, was it intimidating.

The composition of the board was really unusual for that time. Before I stepped on, there were two women and an African American man. That kind of diversity was phenomenal (and sadly still is). So for a change, I wasn't the "first" or the "only," but still my impostor fears came up big time. Not only had I not been on a board before but also this was an industry I had no experience in. Even though I was interested in telecommunications and had done some research about it, I really had very limited knowledge about the business.

During the first few meetings, I didn't say a whole lot, feeling as if I were back in class at Columbia. I didn't really know what I was expected to do. I knew that as a board member you are first and foremost an advisor, but I kept asking myself what I could advise on. I was pretty confident about my marketing experience and knew I should be able to contribute from that standpoint. I just didn't want to be pigeonholed in that way. In a corporation, as a woman, you don't want to be able to speak only about things that relate to women. As an African American, you don't want to be the only one talking about issues of people of color. And I didn't want to be able to speak up only when the subject was marketing; I wanted to feel that I could contribute to the conversation about the business in general.

I actually went back and took out my old accounting books. (Accounting was still not my favorite discipline.) I had been working with profit and loss statements for a while, but I didn't do a lot with balance sheets, or cash flow, or dividend yields. So I didn't feel I fully understood the financial engineering of a corporation.

When you are sitting in that boardroom—especially if you are the new kid on the block—you are not going to interrupt and ask a question when you don't understand something. Everyone else on the SNET board seemed like a veteran to me. I was convinced that they all understood everything, and I felt like I didn't have a clue as to what was going on. As usual, at first I dealt with the feelings by overpreparing. Luckily, after a while I did build up my confidence and began to contribute to board discussions.

I had been on the board for a year when Dan Miglio, SNET's chairman and CEO, brought up the idea of a possible merger. The company was too small to make it on its own in the fiercely competitive market that developed after the breakup of AT&T. Either it could find a company with which to align itself, or it would be in danger of being acquired by a competitor.

The company that emerged as the most likely merger partner was Texas-based SBC Communications. Ed Whitacre, SBC's dynamic CEO, was leading an aggressive expansion strategy, and the deal made good sense for both corporations.

As the details of the merger were worked out, it became clear that only one board member from SNET would make the transition to the board of the new entity. Since I was the new kid on the block, I was certain that I would not be the person staying on. So when Rick Goings, my former boss at Avon, who was now the CEO of Tupperware, called to invite me to sit on his board, I accepted.

Rick had approached me once before, shortly after I had joined SNET, but I had had to decline, because the board at Carson allowed me to sit on only one outside board. Now, when he read the announcement about the merger, Rick decided to try again. "I wanted to get to you first," he said, "before you accepted another board." I was flattered and told him that I would love to join his board.

Imagine my surprise, then, to learn that I had been selected to become one of the directors at SBC after the merger. I was shocked, actually. When Dan called me to give me the news, I explained that, as much as I would have liked to accept, I couldn't, because I had already made a commitment to Tupperware. The next thing I knew, Ed Whitacre was on the phone, asking me to go to the Carson Board to try to convince them to allow me to serve on two outside boards by explaining how the experience on the SBC Board could be of value to Carson.

I took Ed's advice and ended up accepting positions on both boards. Since the SNET-SBC merger didn't close for several months, I started with Tupperware first. At that time, it was not yet common practice to have orientations for new board members. Tupperware was ahead of the times, though, and they gave me a thorough orientation. I met with the chief financial officer, the marketing people, the head of the sales organization, and the head of human resources, and got a really in-depth look at the company's operations and strategic plan.

That really helped me to feel more comfortable stepping into that role. I knew the direct-selling industry. I knew the CEO. And now I had a pretty good understanding of the business. I was still new, and I didn't know any of my colleagues, but I felt that I could contribute from the start. That helped me quiet my impostor fears, even though I was the only African American and one of just two women on the board.

As I was getting ready to start on the SBC board, I wanted to make sure that I wouldn't have that same feeling of being out of my league that I had had when I joined SNET. I was just beginning to learn the telecommunications industry, and I wanted to be as prepared as possible. I asked the folks at SBC to do an orientation for me. They had never done one for a board member before, so they weren't even sure what would be helpful. I told them what had worked well at Tupperware, and they obligingly put one together for me.

Randall Stephenson, who is now the CEO of AT&T (the company into which SBC has evolved), still occasionally teases me about putting him through his paces at the time. He was the comptroller when I joined the board, and it was his responsibility to get me up to speed on the finances of the company. He had prepared a PowerPoint presentation, and apparently, after he was done, I peppered him with questions for nearly an hour. For me, it was all about trying to fill in the gaps I still felt I had in my understanding of the business and in my ability to guide the corporation.

It was an effort, but I pushed myself to get involved as quickly as I could on the SBC board. I still questioned whether I had the smarts to fulfill my role as an advisor, but I figured that if I stayed silent, I was definitely not going to do the job. And as I gained confidence in my ability to ask the right questions—which is a board member's most important responsibility—my worries about deserving the post receded.

When six months later August Busch asked me to consider a position on the Anheuser board, I had a game plan for handling my impostor fears. I knew that they would come up and that I could work through them by preparing myself to make a contribution as quickly as possible. And that's what I have done with every new board position I have accepted.

A Weight Off

The insights I was gaining and the confidence I was building through my experiences as a board member also stood me in good stead in dealing with the challenges of my work at Carson. I felt a whole lot of weight because I was the one with business experience but at the same time was new in the role of a general manager. And I didn't feel like I really had anybody else I could turn to. So the pressure of trying to make good decisions was constant.

The pace at which we were trying to grow made it that much more daunting. We were executing on all the strategies at once. We were now public in South Africa, growing our international business, entering the salon sector, adding a cosmetics line, and consolidating our market segment by buying out competitors.

With all that going on, I was really dismayed to learn that the investors had been in discussions with bankers in the United States about taking the company public on the New York Stock Exchange. Before I signed on with Carson, I had questioned the people at Morningside Capital closely to make sure that they were planning to grow the company and not simply looking to make a quick profit. They had assured me that they were in for the long haul, so I was unpleasantly surprised when I got a call from Roy and Vince while overseas on business to tell me that a stateside initial public offering was in the works.

I was the only one on the management team with experience in working for a publicly traded company, and I knew how demanding the market, especially the U.S. market, was on a business. It is one thing to run into problems as a private company. There is a whole lot more room to make corrections. The market, however, has little appetite for hiccups.

In addition, ours would be classified as a growth stock, which meant that we would be expected to deliver consistently high-growth numbers. We were already straining capacity to meet our ambitious strategic goals. The need to meet the demands of the market would ratchet up the pressure even further.

I expressed my concerns about the initial public offering, noting that we were beginning to have some challenges keeping up with the volume of demand. However, I found myself the lone voice in the wilderness. In retrospect, I believe the investors saw that there was potential for a quick exit strategy and decided to pursue it.

Our stock made its debut on the New York Stock Exchange three months after we had gone public in Johannesburg. It was received well but did not see the kind of jump in price we had seen in South Africa. The first six months after we became public were OK. We were meeting our goals, and our first earnings calls were fine.

Then, in part because of a softening market, and in part

because of operational issues, our growth started to slow. The production challenges we had were definitely affecting sales. Minor problems developed into major setbacks. We missed the target dates for several shipments to Wal-Mart, for example. And that is one thing you just can't afford to do as a consumer products company.

Our domestic business suffered. We were no longer generating the kind of growth the market expected. We were still growing, but now at a rate that was in the very low double digits. We were still growing internationally at over twenty percent, but the analysts tend to be a little skeptical about that kind of growth. They were concerned with the many risk factors inherent in international trade, and discounted our overseas growth. So our stock got hit pretty badly.

We were really under the microscope since we were one of the very few companies on the New York Stock Exchange exclusively focused on the African American market. Even though we weren't minority-owned, we got a lot of attention from the press. So there was an added public element to our struggles, and it felt as if some of the decisions the board was making had more to do with managing public perception than with addressing the underlying problems.

In June of 1998, I was in France to give a speech at the World Perfumery Congress. I had invited my niece Candice along, as well as my childhood friend Barbara and her daughter Phylissia, who is my goddaughter. Phylissia had just graduated from high school and my niece from college. This was a special trip to celebrate these milestones. Neither of the girls nor Barbara had been to Europe before, and we had planned to travel around for several days after I had finished my work.

Vince reached me at the hotel and informed me that Roy would be stepping down as CEO and only maintaining his role as chair. The second-quarter earnings were weak, and the board felt that it was important to show that the company was responding decisively. They wanted me to fly back that night to be on stage when they made the announcement.

I agreed, but something just didn't sit right with me. I called back and said, "Do you really need me there? I've got family with me, and I am going to have to arrange for all four of us to get back on such short notice. It's going to be exorbitantly expensive." We went back and forth a bit but ultimately agreed that my presence wasn't absolutely essential.

When I returned, Vince filled me in on where things stood. He had taken over as interim CEO. I would continue as president, and the company would do a search for a new CEO. Since the challenges we were facing were in part operational, Vince explained, the board didn't think that the market would react well if I were to move into the CEO role.

I wasn't thrilled with the decision but resolved not to challenge it and to see what would happen. I went on with my work, and after about six months, Greg Andrews was named CEO. He was an African American executive who had worked for Colgate. He had been in the ethnic hair care industry for a long time, and I was excited about working together with him to correct some of the problems we were having.

It quickly became apparent, however, that he didn't think he needed a president or a chief operating officer. He made it clear that he wanted complete control. If I made a decision, he made a different decision, and our people got directions from both of us. It was very dysfunctional.

After about three months of trying to work with Greg, I decided that it just was not worth it. I was in the fourth year of my contract, and I didn't want all this angst. If the CEO wanted to run the entire show, it was probably time for me to let him. I informed the company that I was stepping down and left about a month after that.

Feeling Worthy

The most amazing part of my decision to leave Carson was that I did not feel like a failure for walking away. I had developed enough of a sense of self-worth to feel that I could control more of my destiny. I didn't need the external validation as much, and I didn't need to put up with a situation where my skills and expertise weren't appreciated.

In the three and a half years I had been with Carson, I had accomplished enough to be able to give myself validation. I could look in the mirror and say with confidence, "You're a business person." I knew I wasn't leaving because I couldn't cut it, even though I was disappointed not to have been given the chance to help really get the company back on track. So as I left, I did so without carrying any emotional baggage.

It had been such a hectic several years, I felt just completely burned out. The newfound sense of worth allowed me to relax and give myself time to regroup. I realized that for a long while I hadn't felt like I was in control of my life. And I wanted to get me back.

Sooner or later, that is the conversation we all need to have with ourselves: am I in charge of my life? For those of us who suffer from the impostor syndrome, the answer is generally an emphatic "no." Our lives tend to revolve around the need for approval and the endless labor of earning it.

With time, many of us come to recognize that our energies are misdirected. External validation, no matter how much of it we get, only feeds our need for more and the anxiety of not being worthy. And as we turn our attention to learning how to give ourselves validation, we discover how much happier and in control we are.

We also discover, as Susie Buffett so thoughtfully describes, that our relationships with others change. We begin to recognize them as people, with their own needs and foibles. And we allow ourselves to take in the love, respect, and appreciation they offer us, without brushing it aside as something that couldn't possibly be true.

Susie, an ardent supporter of children and of social justice, has served for many years on the Girls Inc. board. I was thrilled to get to know her: she is one of the most genuine, committed, and down-to-earth people I've ever met. And equally as important, she really knows how to have a good time. As Susie explains, that ability to find joy largely comes from having taken the time to sort out what's really important in life.

Susie Buffett: *Sooner or Later, Everything Is Funny*

Several years ago, at a Girls Inc. luncheon where my dad was speaking, he was introduced by one of the girls as "a super famous k-jillionaire. The Oracle of Omaha. Omaha's homeboy." But when I was growing up, he wasn't that well known. Nobody was paying any attention to him until I was in my early twenties, so my childhood was pretty normal.

I am the oldest of three and the only girl. My mother was very involved in the civil rights movement, and often I was right there with her in the community, speaking on panels, volunteering at Head Start, and starting Girls Inc. in a church basement. My dad was very supportive of her work and was extremely pro-women in general. I remember hearing him say to my mother when I was very young, "Wait until women find out they're the real slaves of the world."

I never got the message that as a girl I was supposed to be a nurse, secretary, teacher, or housewife. Even so, during my freshman year at the University of Nebraska, I majored in home economics. And that was back in the old days, when it was cooking and sewing. Then I transferred to the University of California at Irvine, and I enrolled in social ecology. It was an odd combination of disciplines: I was taking classes in Black studies, in criminal justice, and even in statistics.

After college, I decided not to go back to Omaha. I had a great group of friends, and I loved life in California. Although I didn't know what I wanted to be when I grew up, I took a job working at Century 21. Art Bartlett, the founder and CEO, was a pretty driven guy. He had started a little real estate company and grown it into a huge corporation. There were about two hundred franchisees when I started in 1974; there were almost eight thousand when I left in 1980.

Art could be a very demanding person. It's what made him successful, but it could also make him a challenging boss. One day, his assistant quit in tears. I was the only one who was brave enough to go in and answer his phone while he was in meetings all day. No one could believe I was going to do it. Everyone was so afraid of him.

And I thought, "Well, how bad can this guy be? I mean, he's just a guy."

At the end of that first day, Art came out of his office and asked me if I would take the job permanently. I said I would with a few conditions. "I'm not going to cry," I said, "and we always have to talk to each other." He agreed to my conditions, and ultimately we had a great time working together. I learned so much from him. He had never intended to build that company the way he did. It happened by accident, which is what made it fun. (But that's another book!)

I also learned a lot about the judgments we all make about each other based on nothing more than what's on the outside, on our own preconceived notions. One day, I made Art walk around the office and say "hi" to everyone. I thought my coworkers were all going to die. They thought of him as aloof, reserved, and sometimes even a cold man. And I had a totally different view of him, because I'd gotten to know him as a person. Under that hard exterior, he cared deeply about his employees. I loved that man until the day he died in 2009.

When I was about twenty-nine, I moved to Washington, DC, and the lessons about judgments came in handy. I wasn't really sure what I wanted to do and wasn't feeling my most confident.

Again by accident, I ended up in a job that was both intimidating but also great fun. I worked at the *New Republic*. For the most part, all the writers and editors at the magazine were brilliant guys who had graduated from Harvard. People like Charles Krauthammer and Michael Kinsley sitting around and talking politics. It was very interesting, but it also made me feel unsure of myself.

It took about eight months of not only working with these guys but going out to lunch and talking about regular old stuff—not high-level politics or the problems in Israel, but families, children, and weddings—for me to get comfortable. After a while, you recognize that it doesn't matter how many degrees they have or the kind of honors they received, they're all just people. I relaxed and realized that in addition to coworkers, we were also friends.

By that point in my life, my dad had become much more of a public personality, and many people had formed opinions about him. To this day, I can't eat in a restaurant in Omaha without hearing someone discussing my father. Of course, they don't know him and most of the time they don't know what they're talking about. It's just another example of how real people become almost fictionalized characters through the mindless chatter of people, media, tabloids—you name it.

I remember handing my credit card to somebody in a store, and when she saw my name, she said, "Oh, are you related to Warren Buffett?" And when I said "yes," she exclaimed, "You're so lucky."

The woman happened to be right. I am very, very lucky. But I thought, "How do you know that? How do you know what kind of relationship I have with my dad or even what kind of person he is?"

Everybody's just a person. We all have our stories. We all have our struggles. People spend so much time comparing themselves to others and worrying about what other people think. And so much of that stuff just doesn't matter. I feel fortunate that my childhood and my workplace experiences helped ground me. I always knew what mattered.

After my mother died, I thought, "Okay, life is short. How do I want to be spending the rest of my life?"

I was in the fortunate position to be able to make changes in my life. I spend more evenings eating takeout with my friends and fewer evenings at galas and benefits. I wear jeans more and "black tie" never. I say "no" more. I delegate more and don't feel the need to control everything. I still don't want to cry at work, and I want everyone at the office to be able to talk to each other—just like I did at Century 21, when I was twenty-five years old. The important things don't change. I've learned that it's important to let go of the stuff that you can't do anything about. Of course, all this is easy to say. It can be hard to do.

One thing that helps is a sense of humor. Sooner or later, most everything becomes funny.

Life changes dramatically when you begin to acknowledge yourself for your success. It's not that the impostor fears go away entirely; they just become much less insistent. There is suddenly more room to breathe and the quiet space necessary to think about how you want to live.

Chapter 11

Listen to Your Heart

Show up for life as your whole self. Your essence is what makes you who you are. Connecting with that spiritual essence is a critical element in moving toward conquering the impostor syndrome.

Find the quiet place inside where you feel safe to be yourself. From that place, work to clarify your own values and then ask whether the people around you share those values. Build connections with those people who do.

When I left Carson, I knew that I needed to take some time to decide what I wanted to do next. I was in my early fifties now, and while I was certainly not ready to retire, I also recognized that, most likely, I was entering the last phase of my full-time working career. And I wanted to make sure that it would be meaningful and enjoyable.

I had had two such different experiences up to that point: the long period of learning and growth at a large corporation and the short, intense time of building up a small company. I had gotten so much from each, but I was not at all sure that I wanted to return to either. Fortunately, I had the luxury of time and the emotional tools I had acquired in my struggle with the impostor syndrome.

I set myself the task of figuring out what it was I really wanted. In my search for internal validation, I had done a lot of writing to myself in the years leading up to this point, taking inventory of who I was and what I had accomplished. I began by reviewing these lists, to remind myself of the journey that had gotten me where I was. I then expanded the inventory. I was painfully honest with myself about what I was and wasn't good at. I pushed myself to distinguish between the things I liked and those I really didn't like but I pretended to. And most importantly, I thought about what I truly valued in my life.

Through this reflection, it became apparent that proving myself was no longer the sole objective. When I left Avon, what I wanted was another challenge, and everything else—location, industry—was wide open. Now, I wanted not only a professional challenge but also a position that was congruent with who I was as a person. With that, two priorities emerged: I wanted to be with a company (at this point I still thought I would remain in the corporate world) that had really strong values, one that treated people with respect and demonstrated its commitment to its employees and to the community. I also wanted to stay geographically close enough to the people in my life to maintain intimate connections.

My commitment to these priorities was put to the test when I had the opportunity to interview for the head of marketing position at Starbucks. The company not only was a marketing powerhouse but also had a reputation for treating people really well. When I went out to Seattle to interview, it was clear that this reputation was well-earned, and I loved everything about the company. But the job was in Seattle, and that was just too far from everybody who was important to me. I stuck to my guns and did not pursue the opportunity further.

As I was sorting through my professional options, I used some of my spare time to do a bit of pro bono work for a couple of local nonprofit organizations. I had first become engaged with nonprofits, somewhat reluctantly, I must admit, when I was at Avon. Ernesta Procope, the storied African American businesswoman, who was a board member of the company, had recommended me to serve on a corporate advisory board at Queens College. Ernesta and I had met when, upon joining the board, she had insisted on meeting the women of color who were moving up in the company. I didn't have any connection to Queens College and was very concerned about the time commitment, but I was honored to have been singled out by Ernesta and signed on.

The liberal arts college was creating a business minor and was seeking guidance from corporations on the kinds of skills graduates would need. They had assembled a group of really interesting people, many of them Queens College alumni who held high-level positions in New York.

From the start, I found the conversation fascinating. We were discussing the real-life applications of education. Our role was to help the college understand how best to prepare students for successful careers in the business world by sharing our observations of the kinds of skills newly graduated employees tended to lack. It was a really worthwhile effort, and it didn't take a lot of time. I quickly realized that I was getting much more out of this work than the amount of effort it required.

Now, in Savannah, I had much the same experience. I felt that I was making a real contribution and having an impact. Yet it was fairly effortless, and I was getting great satisfaction from the work I was doing with these nonprofits.

As I thought about all this, I heard Aunt Rose say, as she had many times over the course of my growing up, "Joyce Marie, to get where you're going, you've got to be strong enough to listen to your heart." And I wondered whether my heart was telling me something new, pointing me in a direction I had not considered before. Suddenly, I could see myself leaving the corporate world and devoting myself to a social mission that was important to me.

Blazing a New Trail

I was excited by the idea of shifting to the social sector, but felt cautious, because I didn't know of anyone who had made that kind of switch. Before I allowed myself to get too enthusiastic, I wanted to get some expert advice from someone who understood both the corporate and the nonprofit worlds. The person who came to mind was Debra Oppenheim, who had placed me on the SNET board. I knew that Debra's executive search firm worked with both sectors, and I trusted her to give me some guidance.

On my way to New York to meet with another recruiter about a corporate position, I called Debra and asked her to have lunch. After we had caught up a bit, I told Debra what I was thinking about and said, "How strange would it be to try something like this?"

My real concern was that if I tried for a leadership role at a nonprofit, I wouldn't be accepted. Like many corporate people, I had the sense that nonprofits wanted folks like me on their boards but didn't think that we understood what it means to make a real commitment to a cause.

"Are people going to question my passion for the work?" I asked Debra. "Am I going to face a lot of suspicion and resistance because of my background?"

"Well, Joyce," she replied after a pause, "you said it has to be the right organization for you to consider this. I think the right organization would feel lucky to get somebody with your background and experience."

Debra than proceeded to give me the lowdown on some of the realities of working in the nonprofit sector: "You're not going to make the same kind of money. You're not going to have the same kind of resources. And you'll have to do a lot of work that you are probably used to delegating. All that said, as you've discovered, you're going to get a lot from the fact that you are making an impact.

"Now," she continued, "what would be the right organization for you?"

I felt strongly that I wanted to work for an organization whose mission focused either on women's and girls' issues or on education. Through my own experience and those of people whom I had helped along the way in my career, I knew the limitations gender and race could impose on individual development, and I wanted to contribute to counteracting their effects.

Naming what I might want to do and Debra's clear-eyed encouragement helped to shift my emotional posture. As we said goodbye, Debra told me that she would keep her eyes open, and I allowed myself to think seriously about making another big change in my life.

Again the universe surprised me with its agility in responding to my willingness to try something new. Within weeks, Debra called to ask whether I would be interested in looking at the position of president and CEO of Girls Inc. I had to admit that I didn't know the organization. Debra explained that it was the former Girls Clubs of America and gave me a bit of background about the name change that had taken place ten years earlier. She also gave me a brief sketch of the work of the organization, its structure, and its strategic direction.

It sounded very interesting, but I needed a lot more information before I could decide whether I wanted to pursue the opportunity. Debra sent me a large packet of materials, and in the meantime I did some research online. What I read really got me excited. The mission was very stirring: to inspire all girls to be strong, smart, and bold. And the organization itself seemed to be professional, innovative, and deeply respectful of the girls it served.

I was especially intrigued by the business structure of the organization. Girls Inc. is a federated system, which brings together a national office and a network of independent affiliates. The national entity serves a "corporate" function, conducting research, developing programming, maintaining quality standards, and providing marketing support. The affiliates work directly with girls, creating safe, nurturing environments, delivering programs, and offering support and opportunities for growth. In this system, I immediately saw many parallels with the direct-selling distribution structure I knew so well through my many years at Avon. It was heartening to think that my experience could be directly relevant to the work of the organization.

I asked Debra to put my name forth as a candidate for the position. Shortly after, she let me know that the search committee wanted to meet with me. I am not sure what I was expecting when I went back to New York for the interview, but when I walked into the austere conference room and faced the six very serious people, I was really taken aback. It wasn't as if I thought they would have halos around their heads, but I was looking to get a glimpse of the heart of the organization, of the passion that drove it. Instead, it felt like a pretty pro forma interview, with the committee asking a lot of questions about my career and so on. I answered but also tried hard to spark a conversation about the emotional content of the work. And the entire time it felt as if we were working at cross purposes.

"Boy, that was the worst interview I've ever done in my life," I told Debra as we debriefed afterwards. "I don't think this is going to go anywhere."

She encouraged me not to jump to conclusions and to wait for feedback from the committee, but I was fairly convinced that they had felt the same way I did and that there would be no further conversations. With that, I went off to Denver, where I was interviewing to become president of a company that provided advisory services on work–life issues to corporate clients. It was an exciting opportunity in its own right, and now that Girls Inc. seemed like a nonstarter, I was inclined to consider it that much more seriously.

I had a series of great meetings in Denver and was back in Savannah when Debra called me about a week after my interview with the search committee. Much to my surprise, she said, "They really are very, very interested. But their big question is how serious you are about taking a position like this. They want to make sure you are not just fishing."

"Oh, goodness," I said, "Debra, I wouldn't have gone there and wasted everybody's time. I've got to tell you, though, I really didn't see the kind of passion I was looking for, so I don't know how I feel about the opportunity."

We talked some more, and Debra suggested that I meet with a few key people in the organization to see whether there was in fact a spark. I agreed, and a couple of weeks later returned to New York. The first meeting was a breakfast with Frank Burnes, a managing director at JPMorgan Chase, who was the chair of the Girls Inc. board, and Janice Warne, who headed up the search committee. I found them both warm and funny. I clearly saw their commitment to the organization and how passionately they felt about its mission. I also understood what they felt was needed from a business standpoint and why they thought somebody with my skills could be an asset to the organization.

Afterwards, I went down to the Girls Inc. headquarters on Wall Street. Among the many images of girls that adorned the walls, a vibrant multicolored print depicting girls expressing their dreams for the future really struck me. And then, in a sunlit conference room overlooking the East River, I met half a dozen bright, passionate people—the senior management team—who spoke eloquently and movingly about the systematic way the organization went about inspiring girls to dream big and giving them the tools to work toward those dreams. I had read the descriptions of the programs and looked at the service statistics, but now I began to understand the depth of the programming philosophy and the commitment to providing transformational opportunities to every girl who came through the doors of Girls Inc.

I ended the day in Riverside Park, talking with Isabel Carter Stewart, who had stepped down as president of the organization to move to Chicago with her family. The movers were literally packing up the last of the apartment when we met, which gave us an excuse to enjoy a spring day in the park. Isabel was charming and very wise, in a quiet sort of way. We talked for a long time, laughing a lot. When it was time to be on our way, Isabel gave me a quick hug and said, "If you decide to do this, you'll really be doing God's work."

As I reflected on those words over the next few days, a new sense of excitement began to stir. It was a hopeful kind of feeling, an inkling that I had a chance to change my relationship with work. That was thrilling and scary. I knew in my heart that if I made this decision to step away from the corporate world, I would probably never go back. And it is not easy to walk away from twenty-five years of striving and success. My impostor fears also reared up, making me question whether I was up to this job, especially the fundraising part.

I mulled all this over for the next month or so, waiting to hear back from Girls Inc. and the company in Denver. Ironically, both search firms called within hours of each other, each offering me the respective jobs. Of course, it would have been easier if the decision had been made for me, but then it wouldn't have been my decision. This was a chance to question myself closely and to come up with an honest answer about what I wanted to do next. It was an opportunity to listen to my heart.

I told both search firms that I needed a week and started

thinking what I was going to do to come to a decision. I remembered a colleague recommending Skylonda Spa, a mind/body retreat in Northern California, where she had gone to sort out some life concerns. I looked it up online, and it sounded like exactly what I needed, a place to nurture myself while I pondered this big fork in the road.

I booked myself into the spa for a week, and it was just the right thing for me. I hiked, meditated, got massages, ate well, and slept a lot. It was a chance for me to allow my whole being to make the decision rather than my intellect alone. At the end of the week, the answer was clear, and I felt surprisingly light and peaceful.

What I wanted—and now I had the words to articulate the wish—was a feeling of rightness. I wanted to wake up every morning and know with absolute certainty what I was working for. More than anything else, I wanted to have what I did be an expression of who I was.

With that, I called the search firm for the company in Denver and turned down the position, explaining that I had decided to take my career in a new direction. And then I called Debra and told her I wanted to join Girls Inc.

Essential Work

I accepted the job at Girls Inc. in the beginning of the summer of 2000. There were things I needed to wrap up in Savannah, and, of course, I had to move myself back to New York. I negotiated to begin work in September and got busy getting ready for this new chapter of my life.

The move itself was going to be pretty easy. I owned my

apartment in New York and had been leasing it the whole time I was down in Savannah. Now, I just needed to get it all set up and move in.

More than anything else, I wanted time to prepare for this very different kind of challenge. There was so much I didn't know about running a nonprofit organization in general, and there was so much to learn about Girls Inc. in particular. So I read a lot, pored over the organization's strategic plan and its financial statements, and talked to as many people as I could.

There was no hiding the fact that in spite of my years of business experience, I was a novice in the nonprofit world. As the end of the summer approached, I kept expecting the impostor fears to kick up big time. But they never did. I had my concerns, certainly, yet the familiar panic of being a fake just wasn't there. At the time, I didn't consciously articulate what was different. However, as I thought about it in the years since, I have realized that I wasn't worried about being discovered as an impostor because for the first time in my life I was bringing my essential self to work. Even if I failed miserably at the job, it wasn't going to be because I was faking it.

My friend Anne Szostak once told me about a diversity initiative she had led at her corporation. What made it work, she explained, was that "people liked the fact that they could show up to work as their whole selves." Unfortunately, most of us believe that our value lies in our productivity, intelligence, work ethic, etc., and not in our essence. But all of these attributes are pale shadows without the animating force of the spirit that makes each of us who we are.

What I discovered in taking on the challenge of switching to the social sector was that there is a real correlation between the degree to which we bring our whole selves to work and the degree to which we experience the impostor syndrome. Mary Wagner, a dear friend who is senior vice president of global research & development at Starbucks, generously shared what her mother taught her about maintaining a commitment to who you are and how she has used that lesson to overcome self-doubt in her career.

Mary Wagner: *A Lesson in Staying True to Yourself*

When my mom died, at age ninety-two, all of her girlfriends (themselves well into their eighties), kept telling me, "Your mother could have been a CEO anywhere." And she should have been. She was great with numbers and had a real head for business. But she grew up in a different era, in a farming family. Her father dictated that as a woman she could be either a nurse or a teacher. My mother chose to be a teacher. She started her career in a one-room schoolhouse in the Wisconsin town where she grew up and taught for over forty years. And yet she didn't entirely embrace teaching, because it wasn't her true calling.

She never complained about her work, but she raised her three children to pursue our interests seriously. As the oldest girl, I really took after my mother. In high school, I was the kind of person who, as my girlfriends tease me, would have run for president of the Barbie club if there had been one. I was involved in everything and wanted to lead everything. I was in Girls State, and then Girls Nation. I was captain of our cheerleading squad. You name it.

My father had a high school degree, and my mom had attended

a two-year college to get her teaching certificate. In our house, it was not even a question that all of us kids would go to college. The question was what we would study. My brother was getting an industrial engineering degree, and I wanted to be a veterinarian. I did well in school, so this was a realistic goal.

When it came time to apply to college, my mom took a day off work and went with me to see our guidance counselor. He was young and good-looking, and I thought he was what people must have meant when they said "tall, dark, and handsome." He welcomed us into his office, and when we settled in, he asked what my plans for the future might be. When I told him I wanted to be a vet, he looked surprised, and then said, "But Mary, you would be such a pretty nurse."

I could see my mother's strong jaw jut forward just a tiny bit, and then she said, standing up, "Well, thank you for your time. I think we are done here." That was probably the most important lesson I have learned in my life about not letting other people define me.

As it happened, I ended up choosing not to become a vet after I had taken time off from Iowa State University, where I was getting a degree in microbiology, to work for a veterinarian. I just didn't like it enough. Luckily, when I returned to school, I happened to take a class in food science, which I loved. Who knew you could do all these amazing things with chemistry? My professor, the wonderful Alan Kraft, recognized my passion for the work and suggested that I stay on to do a master's in the department. And I was having so much fun learning about all the things that happen when you mix peanut butter and ketchup, I knew this was the right place for me.

But I am my mother's daughter, you know, and I have this drive. So as I was working on my master's, I kept reading about the CEOs of all these companies and noticing that many of them had Ph.Ds.

Seeing that, I decided I'd better get one, too. I spent the next four years at the University of Minnesota, working on my doctorate, and then another year and a half on the faculty of the University of Wisconsin. That was a great job. As part of the Extension program, I traveled the state and did all these radio and TV shows teaching people how to can and preserve food. My absolute favorite was a class I taught up in the north woods. I had about twenty truckers all bring in their deer meat, bear meat, and what have you, and for two days we'd make sausage, salami, jerky. It was fabulous.

After a couple of years, I went into industry, starting in a one-person biotech operation at General Mills but quickly moving over to product development on brands like Betty Crocker, Hamburger Helper, and Gorton's Seafood. I think I am good at what I do, and I am pretty savvy with people. But being a scientist in the corporate environment has often proved to be challenging. I'll never forget an early lesson I got on navigating the power dynamics in a company. I was working on Hamburger Helper, and the marketing person on one of the products decided she didn't want peas in the mix because she didn't like peas. Well, I got angry, and in a meeting said something to the effect of, "I don't like peas, either, but that's not science. Why don't we let the consumers decide?" Afterwards, at the insistent suggestion of my boss, I had to apologize to the product person and her boss.

That lesson was essential when I entered parts of the industry where science and art are at the heart of the business. When I worked at Gallo Winery, Mars, Inc., and then joined Starbucks, I had to learn how to collaborate with people who have decades of experience in the arts of winemaking, chocolate making, and coffee roasting. It was intimidating at first. All I have is a Ph.D, an understanding of food science, and some experience. And those are all good things, but they will never add up to knowing what you know when you've been making wine or chocolate or brewing coffee for twenty years. So I've had to learn to remember what I am really good at, and that's listening to people and synthesizing everything we know to do something a little different, something better.

At times when I've felt like I really wasn't sure I could do something, I've always gone back to a memory from graduate school. I had just taken an organic chemistry test, and I thought I had done horribly. I called up Mom and said, "I don't know if I can do this." And without missing a beat, she said, "Look, you don't have to do it. I just read the ads in the paper and Target needs checkout girls." Well, needless to say, that was all the encouragement I needed. It was so effective because it reminded me that what was important wasn't the one thing that was right in front of me but rather what I wanted to do with my life.

That has also guided me when I have felt myself getting lost in the workplace. Whether it's the politics of a place or the culture, sometimes you find yourself becoming something other than yourself. That's the time to step back and question yourself about who is defining you.

What I have learned to do at moments like these is to connect with what I think of as the fabric of my life—and that's my friends and family. In talking to them, I remind myself of who I am and who I want to be. And I have been extremely fortunate, but also extremely determined, in holding onto people from the entire span of my life, from first grade all the way to today. These are the people who know me as I am, who will take me good, bad, happy, or sad. They are honest with me, no matter what. And, in doing so, they help me to stay true to myself.

A critical element in moving toward conquering the impostor syndrome is connecting with your spiritual—essential—self. I am not talking about religious faith, necessarily, but the sense of belonging to something larger than ourselves we get from tuning into the voices of our hearts and being wholly ourselves in the world.

As Mary describes it, it is the fabric of your life—that which not only mirrors faithfully who you are but also accepts, values, and celebrates you. You are at the center of your life's fabric, and self-acceptance is an essential element in coming to know that you are not an impostor.

Chapter 12

Joy, Zest, and Power

Pay it forward. When we help each other confront the challenges of our lives, we all grow. Just as importantly, the fabrics of our lives become richer and more complex. Share your joy, zest, and power and you will be repaid a thousandfold.

When I walked into the Girls Inc. offices on September 11, 2000, to start my new job, and saw the faces of the girls whose images lined the walls, a thrill went through me. I felt as if I had arrived at the destination toward which I had been traveling for a very long time.

As I settled in my chair, I looked at the painting of a flower in full bloom that the Black Employees Network at Avon had presented to me when I became an officer of the company. It was one of the few things from my previous professional life that I had brought in over the weekend to decorate the office. I studied the familiar pattern of pink petals on a black background and thought back to the outpouring of pride from my colleagues and the sense of responsibility I felt to all the people like me coming up behind me.

I focused on the new feeling of responsibility I now had. With the images of girls' lively, curious faces imprinted on my mind, I took in the knowledge that in this job I was ultimately accountable to the girls. The degree to which I did or did not succeed would directly affect their ability to benefit from the mission of the organization. That was certainly a weighty challenge to take on, and yet it didn't seem to trigger my impostor fears. Somehow, even though I had concerns about the things I didn't know, like nonprofit accounting, I didn't feel that I was overreaching. My heart told me that this was the right place for me, and with that, I didn't have the old familiar panic of having to prove that I belonged.

My newfound equanimity was tested rigorously almost immediately. Girls Inc. operated on an October–September fiscal year, so on day one I was thrown into the process of finalizing the budget for the following year, which the board would have to approve at the upcoming annual meeting. Sandra Timmons, who had served as the chief operating officer for the previous couple of years and as the interim CEO during the transition, briefed me on where things stood with the budget. It was clear that there was serious cause for concern, but it took several more days for me to understand the magnitude of the problem we were facing.

As Sandra and I worked with the management team over the course of the following week to prepare the budget, I began to get a much fuller picture of the organization's financial position. After adopting a far-reaching strategic plan two years earlier, Girls Inc. had aggressively expanded the scope of its work and the infrastructure necessary to support its broader efforts. The organization had done very well in bringing in large grants, diversifying its sources of income, and growing its budget to sustain the expansion.

In 2000, however, the economy was faltering after the collapse of the dot-com bubble, and like all nonprofits Girls Inc. had seen a serious drop in donations. The organization was facing a sizable shortfall of revenue versus expenses. In discussing how to address the situation, I began to comprehend the profound structural differences between the finances of nonprofit and for-profit organizations, especially in access to capital and cash.

As I considered the job and then prepared for it over the summer, I had been looking at annual budget numbers, which had looked very strong. But I didn't fully understand the implications of the accounting rules that governed the presentation of the information and had not focused sufficiently on the fact that Girls Inc. didn't have the safety net of a large endowment or reserves. Now we needed to find a way to address the revenue shortfall, which is no easy task in an environment where you have little direct control over your ability to generate income.

I felt a great deal of weight as I realized how delicate the financial stability of the organization could be. And I wouldn't be honest if I said that some impostor fears didn't show up at that point. I was the one coming in with the business skills. But could I keep the organization from hitting a big hiccup on my watch?

When I began to feel that panic, I turned to my trusted technique of analyzing the situation on paper. As usual, this allowed me to think more clearly and to separate out the emotions from the reality. In doing so, I realized that something fundamental had changed. In the past, when I encountered a problem, I would always work to solve it quietly on my own and make it appear as if it had never been that much of an issue. Now, I felt that I didn't have to carry the weight alone. We had real challenges, and I needed to be open about what they were. Ultimately, this was really not about me and my abilities.

I worked with Frank Burnes, our chair, and with the folks on the finance committee to explore possible solutions. Together, we presented the facts to the full board and came to an agreement about the budget for the coming year. It felt incredibly liberating to be able to focus honestly on what needed to be done and not worry about playing politics. All the board members were really supportive and unshakable in their commitment to Girls Inc. It was not an easy introduction to my new role, but one that helped strengthen my conviction that I had made the right decision.

A Journey of Rediscovery

I knew that to make a real contribution to the organization I would have to understand its DNA. Inspiring all girls to be strong, smart, and bold is a great mission. But I needed to know what it meant on a day-to-day basis. How did the programs put it into action? Who were the people doing the work? And what did the girls make of it?

From the start, I made it a point to visit as many affiliates as I could. Some invited me to speak at their fundraisers. Others welcomed me when other business brought me to their communities. Still others were pleased to have me drop in and just visit. It was a remarkable time. I traveled to dozens of towns, large and small, all across the country—from Waterbury, Connecticut, where the first Girls' Club opened its doors in 1864, to Los Angeles, where Girls Inc. was in the process of establishing a foothold.

Everywhere I went, people greeted me with warmth and enthusiasm. They were eager to share their ideas, discuss their concerns, and talk about how together we could all do even more for girls. Most of all, they wanted to show me how they were making a difference in the lives of the girls in their communities.

In buildings of every size and description, I saw girls, from six-year-olds to young ladies of eighteen, engaged in an amazing range of activities. They scaled walls on ropes courses, designed and built robots, took apart car engines, made videos about issues important to them, played tackle football, dissected frogs, and supported each other through the growing pains of adolescence. In all of this, the girls were encouraged and guided by adults who clearly cared about them and wanted them to succeed. It was a real inspiration to observe this powerful community in action, and an honor to know that I was now a part of it.

The conversations I had with the hundreds of girls I met touched me most profoundly. As we spoke and I heard about their lives, I began to recognize myself in them. Many were girls of color. More often than not, their families had very limited financial means. A great many would be the first in their families to go to college, and some would be the first to finish high school.

It also became clear that girls still had to confront not only societal messages that told them they were "less than" but also real obstacles to pursuing their interests. The overt racism and sexism with which I had grown up had been replaced by more subtle, but still insidious, forms of discrimination.

One story I heard that first year left a particularly deep impression. At an event for Girls Inc. of Alameda County, in the San Francisco Bay Area, I heard a teenaged girl named Trang speak about her experience with math. She explained that she loved math and was really good at it. A year or so earlier, though, she had started having a problem in math class. When the teacher asked a question, she would raise her hand, but the teacher would not call on her. In fact, he would mostly call on the boys in the class. Trang started getting discouraged. Her confidence began to erode. She stopped raising her hand. Even her grades began to slip. She knew it wasn't fair, but she didn't know what to do.

Trang turned to her community at Girls Inc. With the help of a staff member and her friends, she found the courage to speak up. She approached the teacher one day after class and asked him why he never called on her when she raised her hand. The teacher was genuinely taken aback; he had not realized that he had been overlooking Trang. Fortunately, he was responsive and mended his ways. Trang's grades were back up to the top of the class, and she was enjoying her favorite subject again.

Trang's story offered a very stark illustration of how our self-image and performance suffer when we perceive that we may not fit in or are not really welcome. What really captured my attention and stirred my heart, however, was the way in which this young girl was able to find enough strength to ask for help and to assert her right to be recognized.

I thought back to the time when I was Trang's age and

had begun to feel not quite good enough. My family could not provide me with the validation I needed to feel comfortable in the places I was reaching for. For Trang, Girls Inc. served that function. It provided the external support necessary to help her develop the skills of internal validation.

When I understood that, I understood the real meaning of strong, smart, and bold. In Girls Inc., girls discover their worlds and who they are. They give voice to their dreams, define their values, and explore possible paths to the future. Most importantly, though, they learn to recognize their own worth, to find a place to stand in the world, and to advocate for themselves and their communities.

To be able to support hundreds of thousands of girls in this way did indeed feel like doing God's work. And that was a different kind of success than I had ever experienced. It came with a sense of peace and elation, and it was wonderfully self-sustaining. All I had to do was do my work.

After the Towers Fell

September 11, 2001, was my first anniversary at Girls Inc. Our offices on Wall Street were just a few blocks away from Ground Zero. Once the scope of the tragedy became apparent that morning, we evacuated and, along with tens of thousands of other shocked New Yorkers, walked away from the smoke and ash that were blanketing the Financial District.

For the first few hours and days, there were the essentials to attend to. We had to make sure everyone was safe and to establish a way of communicating with each other. We also had to let all our board and our colleagues around the country know that we were all right. And we had to find a way to continue to function, so that we could begin the work of figuring out what came next.

We were away from the office for nearly two weeks. As the days passed and we began to get a glimpse of the new world we now lived in, I realized that the biggest challenge Girls Inc. would face would be a financial one. Relief and recovery efforts would be at the front and center of people's minds—and rightfully so—and it would be extremely difficult to raise funds for organizations such as ours.

I had no answers and was worried sick about how we were going to secure the future of Girls Inc. And at the same time, I felt more blessed than ever to be where I was in my life. I had such a deep commitment and sense of obligation to the girls and the organization, and I wanted to do everything in my power to ensure that Girls Inc. would survive and thrive.

In spite of the fear I felt, I was aware of the power that I did have at my disposal. I was part of a community of smart, dedicated people, and, upon reflection, I was confident that I had the skills to lead that community. The conversations I was having with myself during this time were no longer about whether I could do it but rather about what I had to do.

I believe that the fact that I knew how to manage the impostor syndrome by this point made me a much more effective leader. I rallied the staff, the board, and our supporters, and together we found a way to move forward through the difficult couple of years that followed. We had to make painful choices about how much we could take on, but we never compromised in making sure that the girls who attended Girls Inc. had a chance to benefit from thoughtful programming and the nurturing support of well-trained staff.

With time, we began to recover and to focus on growth again. We cultivated affiliates in communities where Girls Inc. did not have a presence, developed new programs, mounted public education campaigns to advocate for gender equity, and forged strategic partnerships with foundations and corporations. The stature and influence of the organization was also growing, and we were able to touch the lives of more and more girls.

I was deeply satisfied with my work and with my personal life at this point. Much to the surprise of most of my friends and family, Johnie and I got married in 2004. We still lived in different cities, so that part of our relationship would not change, but there was something very nice about this change in status.

The following year, Ellyn Spragins approached me about contributing to her book, and I had the opportunity to reflect on what I had learned over the years and to acknowledge the things that really mattered in life. What I discovered was that I wished that I had had the kind of support girls get at Girls Inc., so that I could have been strong, smart, and bold enough to enjoy my professional success much earlier in life. It was really amazing to see how my journey had brought me full circle to where I needed to be.

Stepping Out of the Shadow of Doubt

The impostor syndrome tends to rob those of us who struggle with it of the enjoyment of our success and of a deeper fulfillment for a long time. That in itself is bad enough. However, in doing so, it also keeps many of us from being fully ourselves. We are too busy worrying that other people will question our credentials or our smarts to step out and express who we really are. That way, the impostor syndrome robs our organizations and communities of the benefit of our wholehearted participation.

As Drs. Clance and Imes explained it, when we overcome our fears of being impostors, we begin to experience the "joy, zest, and power" of our accomplishments. That, in turn, empowers us to give more of ourselves. None of us knows for sure what our full potential is, and it is a real disservice to ourselves and to society if we allow self-doubt to keep us from finding out.

Sandra Timmons, who, after leaving Girls Inc. in 2003 went on to become the president and CEO of A Better Chance, speaks very passionately about the social importance of helping young people confront impostor fears. The mission of A Better Chance is to open doors of educational opportunities to young people of color. Since 1963, the organization has helped thousands of young men and women to become educated at some of the nation's top independent schools.

Sandra shares her own experience with the impostor syndrome and her perspective on how it affects young people's performance and participation.

Sandra Timmons: *Out of Place at Five*

I've been fortunate to hear Massachusetts Governor Deval Patrick, who is an alumnus and a dedicated supporter of A Better Chance, tell many moving stories about his life and career. One that never fails to bring tears to my eyes is about his returning home to the South Side of Chicago for the Christmas holidays after the first semester away at prep school. When he arrived, his sister declared that he talked like "a white boy." His grandmother came to his defense, asserting that he spoke like "an educated boy." In that instant, Governor Patrick explains, he realized just how difficult it would be to travel between his two worlds.

I find this particular story so resonant because navigating between their home lives and their school lives is still a major issue for many of our students. I also know personally how lonely and confusing it is to feel that you don't really fit in either place.

My family moved from Johnstown, Pennsylvania, to a military base in Germany when I was three. We returned two years later, but I never felt like Johnstown was supposed to be my home. It was as if I had said, "OK. We are back here for a little while, but then we are going somewhere else." I may have been five when I got back, but I had seen a bit of the world. I knew that there was more than just what this small, industrial city of steel mills had to offer. So part of me always felt like a square peg in a round hole.

I was interested in engineering and science, and when it came time for college, I wanted to go to the General Motors Institute, where you got a degree and then went to work for GM. When I didn't get in, I sort of found myself at loose ends. My parents were telling me to get my act together to apply to other schools, but they were not offering a whole lot of guidance. And I was really struggling. So when a recruiter from the FBI came to the assembly at my high school, I filled out an application. In a few weeks, I got a letter back with a provisional offer of a job upon graduation.

I accepted the job and in the spring of 1978 moved down to Washington, DC to work as a file clerk at the FBI. I was seventeen and earning $7,035. Very quickly, though, I realized that being a file clerk would drive me out of my mind. People would come with a stack of tissue papers two feet high and tell you to put them in alphabetical order and then go and put them in the files. And I wanted to know, "For how long?" Of course, the answer was, "This is what you do." Well, that wasn't going to work for me. I took a class the Bureau offered in fingerprint analysis and moved into the fingerprint unit. I did that for a little over a year, and then realized it was time for college.

My mother, who had been very supportive the whole time, telling me that it was my life and I needed to find my way, said at this point, "You come home, and we'll help you go to school." And that's what I did, enrolling at the Johnstown campus of the University of Pittsburgh.

Having worked for nearly two years before I got to college, I knew what I did and didn't want to do. I majored in business and economics, with a concentration in accounting. And I was a pretty serious student. I'd play around, but only after I got my work done. Even so, I can't say that I was really applying myself intellectually. I just wanted to get the degree, so I could get a better job, get married, and get on with my life.

Heading into the summer after my junior year, I didn't have a job. A family friend who was a professor at the university suggested that I apply for a program that helped prepare you for graduate school. Well, I hadn't thought of graduate school, but I needed something to do, and the program paid a stipend of a thousand dollars. As it happened, I didn't get into that program, but instead was offered a spot in the Quantitative Summer Skills Institute. I was disinclined to go, because the program paid your expenses but didn't offer a stipend. But it was better than sitting around the house all summer.

The Institute, which was funded by the Sloan Foundation and held at Carnegie Mellon University, was designed to encourage students of color to pursue graduate study in the public and nonprofit sectors.

We took courses and learned about public policy. And at the end of the program, the foundation paid for us to apply to six graduate schools to increase our chances of getting accepted.

The Institute—particularly being among this group of smart, competitive students of color who were trying to get into graduate school—was a game changer for me. We all challenged each other, and we all grew as a result. That's when my focus started to shift, when I began to think that I could aspire to more.

I went back to Pitt for my senior year a new person. I brought with me twelve credits for the work I had done over the summer, and I was now on a trajectory to graduate school. There was a consortium of public policy schools that worked with the program, and we were invited to apply to these schools by virtue of being Sloan Fellows.

Carnegie Mellon expressed a strong interest in having me come there, and I accepted a fellowship to go to the university's Graduate School of Urban and Public Affairs to study public policy, with a focus in finance. Going in, I still didn't have a clear idea of what I would do. I thought that I would go to work in a city agency or as an urban planner.

That time of transition, when I allowed myself to believe that I could do something more than just get a job as an accountant and settle down, was in many ways the most terrifying. First of all, you are not sure you can do this. And then the scary question becomes, "If I can't do it, what happens? Where do I go back to?"

I remember one of my first graduate school exams. It was a test with all these graphs and tables, and you were asked to interpret them and explain what they meant. I had always thought I was a good writer and that I had strong critical thinking skills. Well, I got the thing back, and I had done as badly as you could have done without failing outright. For a second, I thought I just couldn't make it. But then I considered the alternative, and that gave me the extra fuel to apply myself in a different way. I realized that I had to work as hard as I could to succeed, because I couldn't go back.

Once I settled into the work and began to do well in graduate school, I began to relax and to realize that I had found my place. That was the first time I felt I was in a community where the people were just like me. And I started to think that maybe I was not a square peg in a round hole after all.

Now, working with our students at A Better Chance, I try to let them know that we understand how difficult it is to feel that you don't belong and how great the temptation is to conform to the group you are with. It can be heartbreaking to watch kids struggle with these issues. For some, the conflict is too great, and they slip away into the protective shell of a manufactured persona. Most, however, find the strength to tolerate the discomfort for a time. It might take a few years and a couple of tries, but invariably, they do find the right place. And that's where they blossom.

The quote attributed to Ralph Waldo Emerson famously says that to succeed is "to laugh often and much... to win the respect of intelligent people... to hear the appreciation of honest critics and endure the betrayal of false friends... to appreciate beauty, to find the best in others: to leave the world a bit better whether by a healthy child, a garden patch, or a redeemed social condition...."

Each of us must define our goals and purpose for ourselves. Yet, the degree to which we become the people our hearts tell us we are is a universal measure of success. To experience the joy, zest, and power of your accomplishments is to succeed greatly.

Afterword

Strategies for Confronting the Impostor Syndrome and Embracing Success

My motivation for writing this book was the wish to help people, especially those in early or mid-career, to overcome impostor fears and embrace their accomplishments and success. I hope that my story and insights, and those of the wonderful folks who shared their experiences in the book, have reassured you that you are not alone and have given you some concrete ideas for beginning to challenge the voices that whisper that you are not good enough and don't deserve to be where you are.

To assist you in developing your own strategies for confronting impostor fears, I have summarized here the tools that the many people with whom I have now spoken about the impostor syndrome have shared with me. You will hear from some of the folks who shared stories in earlier chapters, as well as others who have been willing to share their techniques for conquering self-doubt to embrace their success. You will also find some encouragement and advice to help you on your way. I wish you much success, peace of mind, and enjoyment.

⁂

- Don't stay silent. Find a way to speak about your fears with a trusted friend, a coach, a mentor, your partner, a therapist, or in a journal.

- Get a reality check. Test whether your way of seeing yourself and your abilities and accomplishments is realistic.

- Become familiar with your impostor. What are you trying to prove? To whom? And why?

- Listen to your heart. Work to clarify your own values and build connections with people who share those values.

- Question your work habits. Ask whether all your hard work is making you feel less like a fake. Then, begin to consider what makes you feel truly worthy in your own eyes.

- Get centered in yourself. Don't give power to assumptions other people may make about you.

- Analyze your success. Develop a written inventory of your skills, accomplishments, and experiences to understand your success.

- Know your fear. Learn to distinguish between the stress of moving up into new levels of responsibility and influence and the conditioned response of impostor fears.

- Build self-awareness. Practice looking at your strengths and challenges as a whole person; don't overestimate one or the other.

- Learn to metabolize external validation. The next time someone compliments you on something you have done well, put aside your habitual response and allow the information to sink in.

- Ask whether you are satisfied. Consider how satisfied you are with your life, and if you aren't, make a change.

- Recognize people for who they are. Practice seeing other people as they are, with their own needs and foibles. See their strengths and weaknesses.

- Exercise your sense of humor. Try to keep a sense of perspective and to laugh as often as possible—especially at yourself.

- Show up for life as your whole self. Connect with your spiritual essence.

- Pay it forward. Share your joy, zest, and power.

"You have your own special strengths. Measure yourself on how you use them to make a contribution."

> **Val Ackerman**, founding president of the WNBA and former president, USA Basketball

"I say, first of all, don't be afraid to go and talk to a professional about the way feeling like an impostor is affecting your life. And put people around you who can reinforce that you have a right to be where you are. You're just as smart. You're just as good. People who can see what you cannot see, that you do belong."

> **Dr. Ella Edmondson Bell**, associate professor of business administration, Tuck School of Business at Dartmouth

"I've lived long enough with these feelings to say with some conviction that no matter how fearful you are about your job, the sky is not going to fall, you're going to make it, there's going to be a tomorrow. And it's really important to master the skills of positive self-talk."

> **Bernice Bennett**, former assistant vice president, National Association of Public Hospitals and Health Services

"You've got to remember that we are all just people. Even the big scary guys you are sitting at the table with were two years old once. Back then somebody might have been mean to them on the playground. Or their wives might have yelled at them that morning for not taking out the garbage. It's a whole lot easier to feel OK about yourself if you don't lose sight of other people's humanity."

> **Susan A. Buffett**, chair, The Sherwood Foundation

"I think it's important to ask: Do I feel good here? Do I like being in this group? Is this where I fit? Do I shine here? That's how we stay centered."

> **Eileen Fisher,** founder and chief creative officer, Eileen Fisher, Inc.

"Having experienced the impostor syndrome has helped me to be much more sensitive as a manager and a coach. I work really hard to have strong relationships with the people I work with. I believe that it's important that there is no gap between the person that goes home at night and the one who comes to work in the morning."

> **Rick Goings**, chair and CEO, Tupperware Brands

"It's about trusting your inner self, listening to yourself. That's what it took me nearly fifteen years to work out, to learn to listen to myself.

"And then you've got to find a way to communicate what you are feeling and thinking to other people, and how to do it with integrity, in a way that really gets across who you are."

> **Yvonne Jackson**, president, BeecherJackson, Inc. and former chief people officer and senior vice president, corporate human resources, Pfizer, Inc.

"You must believe in a power greater than yourself. You have to have a place where you go at the end of the day and let your inner voice guide you and keep you strong. It's not about religious belief. But you need to believe in something."

> **Paula Banks Jones**, former president, BP Amoco Foundation, and senior vice president for global diversity, PepsiCo

"You need to have a group of people you can talk to. A place you feel comfortable and free to speak about your doubts or questions. In that kind of environment, you let each other know there are no dumb questions, that it's all just a matter of learning."

> **Debra Lee**, chair and CEO, BET Networks

"There's social bias that kids observe from a very early age. And then they internalize it, and it becomes a reality for them.

"So when I talk to young people, I always say: 'Be aware. Be aware of the fact that you're going to have this voice in your head trying to convince you of things that are not true about you.'"

    Angel R. Martinez, chair, CEO and president, Deckers Outdoor Corporation

"When you feel like an impostor, people will tell you, 'You did this really well,' and you are likely to just brush the praise aside, because you don't think you deserve it. That way you miss out on connecting with that other person. You're not only denying yourself, you are dismissing them. It's important to remember that the quality of mercy is twice blessed."

    John Morgan, chair and CEO, Winmark Corporation

"There's nothing more demoralizing than to feel powerless in situations. People think the system holds all the power and they really don't. For me, the turning point was the discovery of my personal power. I began to share my unique experience, the part of me that I had worked so hard to keep in the shadows, and people I held in such high regard began to seek me out for my point of view. And that's when it clicked that I have nothing to be afraid of or concerned about. I started to blossom when I fully understood and began to appreciate my personal power."

    Ron Parker, retired chief global diversity and inclusion officer and senior vice president of human resources and labor relations, PepsiCo

"Without an outside perspective, you're left with your own self-doubt, and the story just gets bigger and more real. All we hear are those tapes we play, 'I can't do this. They're going to find out.'"

> **Rosina Racioppi**, president and CEO, WOMEN
> Unlimited, Inc.

"One of the things that I did over the years that really helped to boost my confidence was a lot of community service. First of all, I just believe in contributing in that way. But also, taking on such projects gave me opportunities to develop my leadership skills and to excel outside of my own organization. So it was another validation of my abilities."

> **Anne Szostak**, president and CEO, Szostak Partners LLC
> and former executive vice president, FleetBoston Financial

"Honor yourself for who you are. There is a place where you belong and where you will be truly valued. It takes faith and time to find it."

> **Sandra Timmons**, president, A Better Chance

"You've got to ask yourself what's the worst thing that can happen if you don't succeed. When you answer that question honestly, you stop sweating the small stuff and begin to realize that you can walk away from whatever situation you are in. With that, you start to look at your life differently, and the freedom you gain is unbelievable."

> **Mary Wagner**, senior vice president of global research and
> development, Starbucks Corporation

"It's important to understand that the impostor syndrome is not an issue that only affects the isolated experiences of some people but is rather a social phenomenon that is potentially marginalizing future leaders. Therefore, it is something that we must strive to understand and address."

Dr. Katherine G. Windsor, head of school, Miss Porter's School

Acknowledgments

We are most deeply grateful to the courageous, generous, caring people who shared their personal experiences of the impostor syndrome: Val Ackerman, Dr. Ella Edmondson Bell, Bernice Bennett, Susan A. Buffett, Eileen Fisher, Rick Goings, Yvonne Jackson, Paula Banks Jones, Debra Lee, Angel R. Martinez, John Morgan, Ron Parker, Rosina Racioppi, Anne Szostak, Sandra Timmons, Mary Wagner, Janice Warne, Edward Whitacre, Jr., and Dr. Katherine G. Windsor. Their wisdom and honesty vastly enriched this book, and our conversations made the process of writing a true joy.

Dr. Pauline Clance was an invaluable guide and advisor in helping understand the impostor syndrome in all its complexity.

Family and friends, far and wide, contributed their support, enthusiasm, memories, honest feedback, gentle understanding, and hot meals to sustain the long creative process.

Jessica Papin of Dystel and Goderich Literary Management has been a thoughtful, candid reader and an unflagging advocate.

Finally, the entire team at Berrett-Koehler have been an inspiring example of mission-driven publishing. This has been a sincere, respectful collaboration.

Thank you.

Index

Joyce M. Roché

As a trailblazer in the corporate world for 25 years, Ms. Roché mentored women by encouraging them to find their voices and take bold career risks to excel. Her vision for empowered businesswomen carried over into her work on behalf of girls when, in 2000, she assumed the role of president and CEO of Girls Inc., the nonprofit organization whose mission is to inspire all girls to be strong, smart, and bold.

Before joining Girls Inc., Ms. Roché served as president and chief operating officer of Carson Products Company, and vice president of global marketing at Avon Products, Inc. While at Avon, Ms. Roché broke new ground, becoming Avon's first African American female vice president, the first African American vice president of marketing, and the company's first vice president of global marketing.

Ms. Roché has received widespread acclaim for her achievements in the business world: In 1998, *Business Week* selected her as one of the "Top Managers to Watch," and in 1997 she was featured on the cover of *Fortune.* In 2006, she received the Legacy Award during *Black Enterprise* magazine's "Women of Power Summit," and in 2007 she received the Distinguished Alumna Award from Columbia University Women in Business.

Ms. Roché is a graduate of Dillard University in New Orleans and holds an MBA from Columbia University. She has successfully completed Stanford University's Senior Executive Program and holds honorary doctorate degrees from Dillard University and North Adams State College. She currently sits on the board of directors of AT&T Inc., Macy's Inc., Tupperware Brands, Dr. Pepper Snapple Group Inc., and the Association of Governing Boards. She is the chair of the board of trustees for Dillard University.

Alexander Kopelman

Mr. Kopelman is a writer and advocate committed to social justice and individual empowerment. He is the author and coauthor of nine other books, including *From Rage to Reason: My Life in Two Americas*, in collaboration with Janet Langhart Cohen, television personality; *What Mama Taught Me*, in collaboration with Tony Brown, host of Tony Brown's Journal on PBS; and *The Miracles of Mentoring*, in collaboration with Thomas W. Dortch, Jr., national chairman of The 100 Black Men of America, Inc.

Mr. Kopelman has a degree in English literature from Vassar College and an MBA in marketing from New York University. He is the founding president of the Children's Arts Guild, Inc., a nonprofit organization dedicated to supporting boys in building social and emotional skills through the active exploration of creativity and the arts.

Berrett–Koehler
Publishers

Berrett-Koehler is an independent publisher dedicated to an ambitious mission: *Creating a World That Works for All.*

We believe that to truly create a better world, action is needed at all levels—individual, organizational, and societal. At the individual level, our publications help people align their lives with their values and with their aspirations for a better world. At the organizational level, our publications promote progressive leadership and management practices, socially responsible approaches to business, and humane and effective organizations. At the societal level, our publications advance social and economic justice, shared prosperity, sustainability, and new solutions to national and global issues.

A major theme of our publications is "Opening Up New Space." Berrett-Koehler titles challenge conventional thinking, introduce new ideas, and foster positive change. Their common quest is changing the underlying beliefs, mindsets, institutions, and structures that keep generating the same cycles of problems, no matter who our leaders are or what improvement programs we adopt.

We strive to practice what we preach—to operate our publishing company in line with the ideas in our books. At the core of our approach is stewardship, which we define as a deep sense of responsibility to administer the company for the benefit of all of our "stakeholder" groups: authors, customers, employees, investors, service providers, and the communities and environment around us.

We are grateful to the thousands of readers, authors, and other friends of the company who consider themselves to be part of the "BK Community." We hope that you, too, will join us in our mission.

A BK Business Book

This book is part of our BK Business series. BK Business titles pioneer new and progressive leadership and management practices in all types of public, private, and nonprofit organizations. They promote socially responsible approaches to business, innovative organizational change methods, and more humane and effective organizations.

Berrett–Koehler Publishers

A community dedicated to creating
a world that works for all

Visit Our Website: www.bkconnection.com

Read book excerpts, see author videos and Internet movies, read
our authors' blogs, join discussion groups, download book apps, find
out about the BK Affiliate Network, browse subject-area libraries of
books, get special discounts, and more!

Subscribe to Our Free E-Newsletter, the *BK Communiqué*

Be the first to hear about new publications, special discount offers,
exclusive articles, news about bestsellers, and more! Get on the list
for our free e-newsletter by going to **www.bkconnection.com**.

Get Quantity Discounts

Berrett-Koehler books are available at quantity discounts for orders
of ten or more copies. Please call us toll-free at (800) 929-2929 or
email us at bkp.orders@aidcvt.com.

Join the BK Community

BKcommunity.com is a virtual meeting place where people from
around the world can engage with kindred spirits to create a world
that works for all. **BKcommunity.com** members may create their own
profiles, blog, start and participate in forums and discussion groups,
post photos and videos, answer surveys, announce and register for
upcoming events, and chat with others online in real time. Please join
the conversation!